THE BEST JAZZ PIANO SOLOS EVER

80 Classics from Miles to Monk, and More!

ISBN 978-1-61774-102-9

HAL•LEONARD®
CORPORATION

7777 W. BLUEMOUND RD. P.O. BOX 13819 MILWAUKEE, WI 53213

Visit Hal Leonard Online at
www.halleonard.com

CONTENTS

AFTERNOON IN PARIS

By JOHN LEWIS

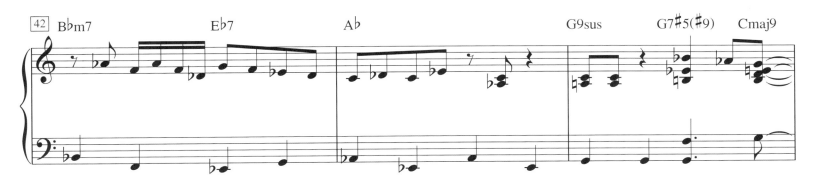

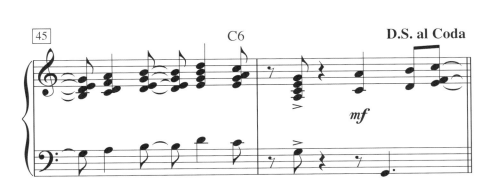

ALLEN'S ALLEY

By DENZIL DeCOSTA BEST

Moderate Latin groove

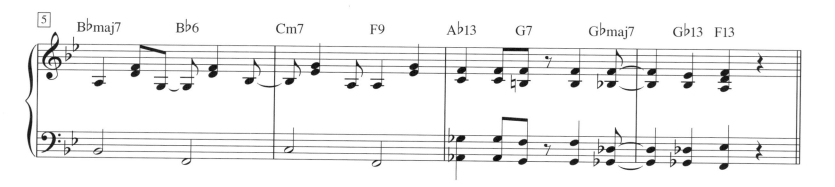

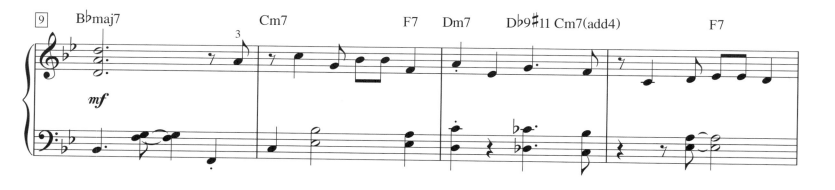

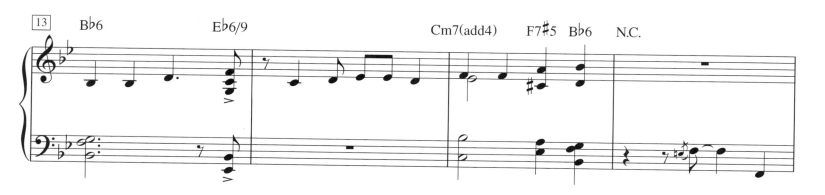

ALONG CAME BETTY

By BENNY GOLSON

15

AZURE-TE
(Paris Blues)

Written by BILL DAVID
and DON WOLF

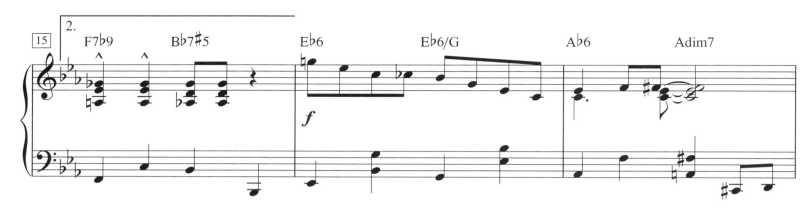

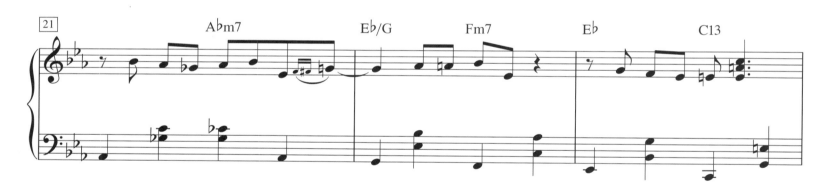

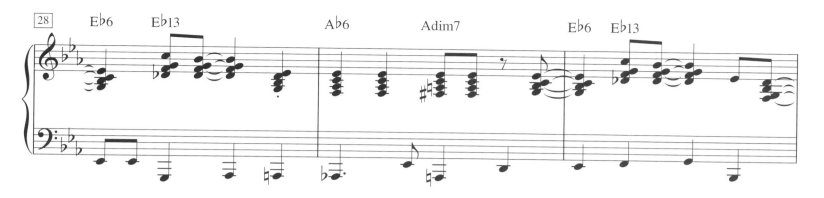

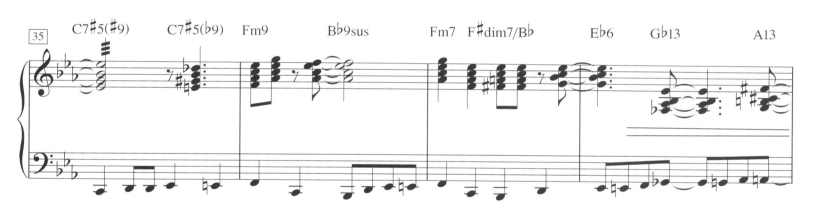

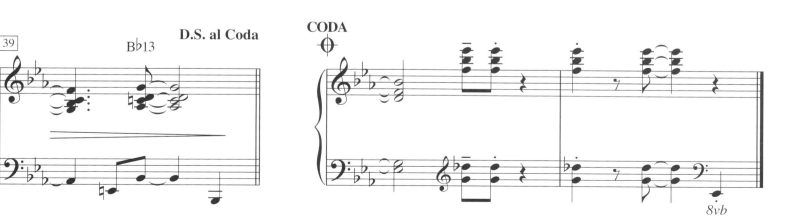

BACK HOME BLUES

By CHARLIE PARKER

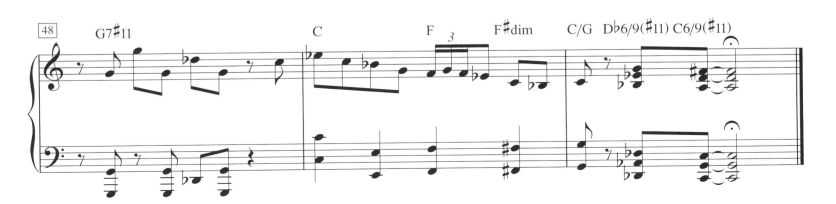

BAGS AND TRANE

By MILT JACKSON

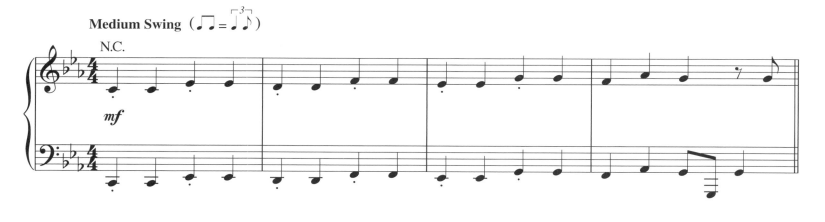

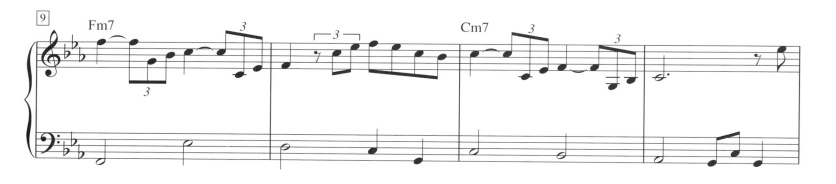

BAGS' GROOVE

By MILT JACKSON

28

BAIA
(Bahía)

Music and Portuguese Lyric by ARY BARROSO
English Lyric by RAY GILBERT

BERNIE'S TUNE

Music by BERNIE MILLER

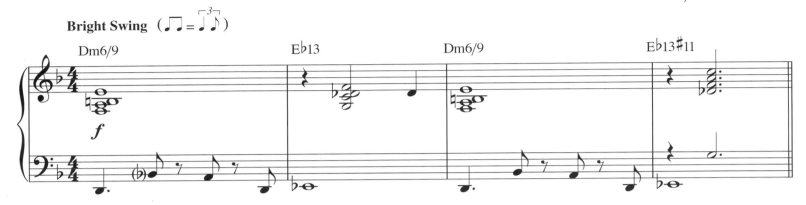

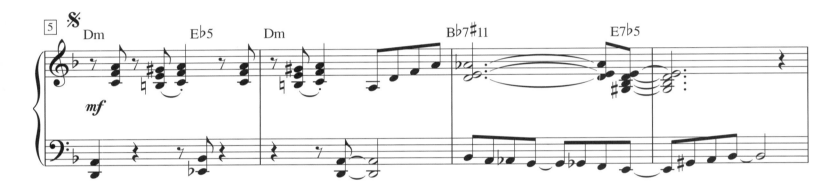

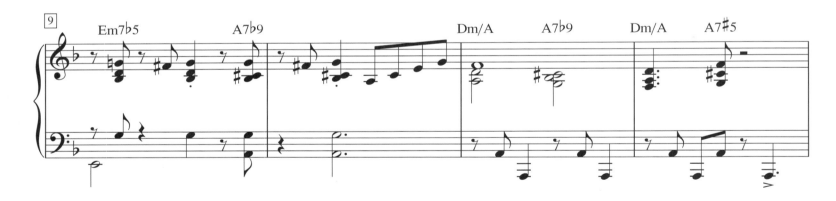

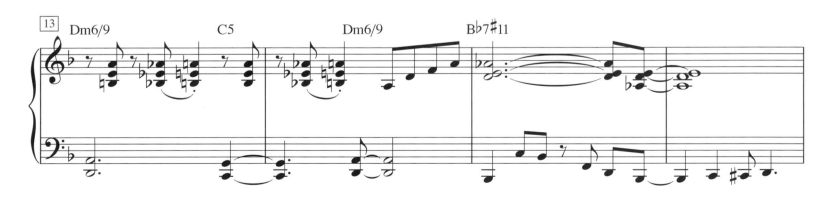

BILLIE'S BOUNCE
(Bill's Bounce)

By CHARLIE PARKER

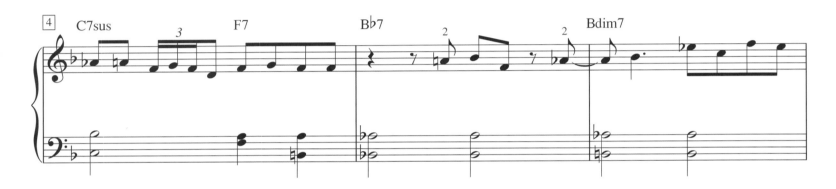

BIRDLAND

Music by JOSEF ZAWINUL

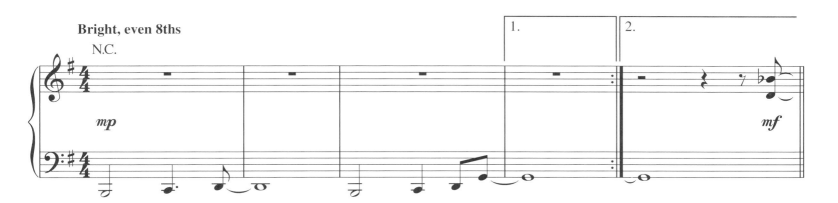

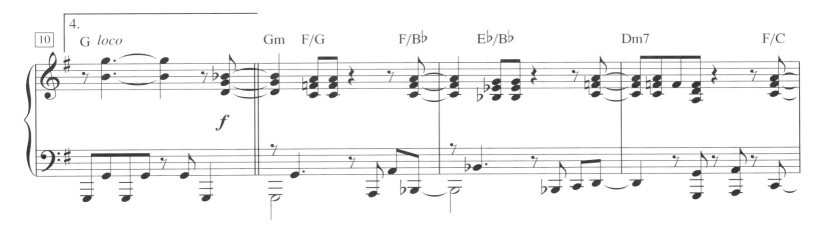

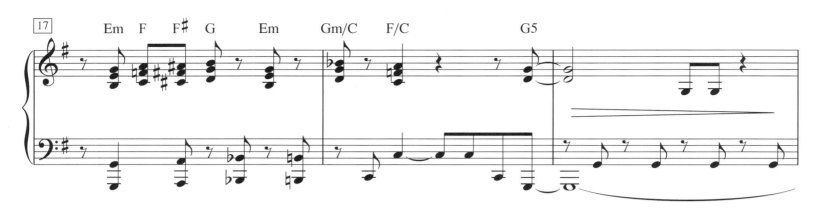

45

BIRK'S WORKS

By DIZZY GILLESPIE

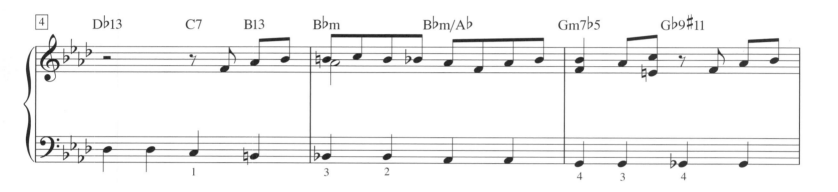

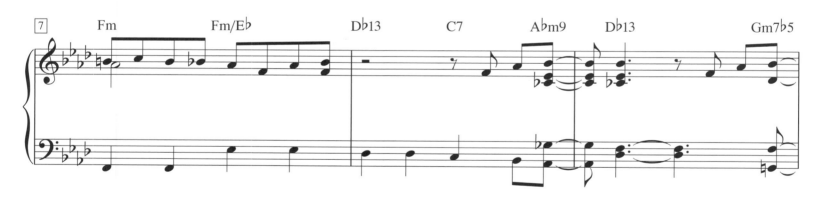

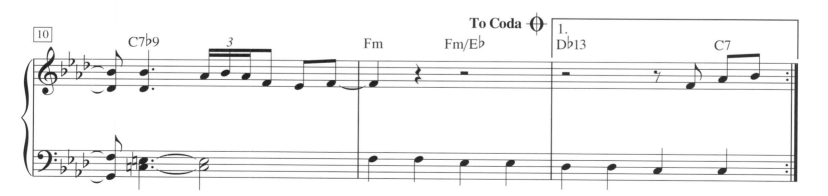

CLOSE YOUR EYES

By BERNICE PETKERE

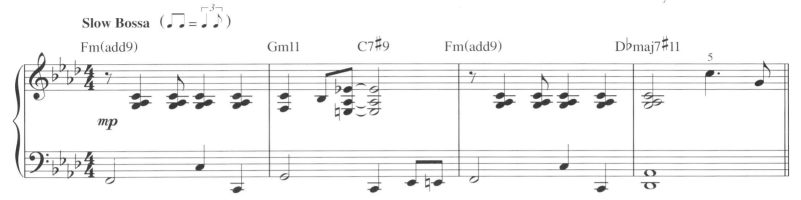

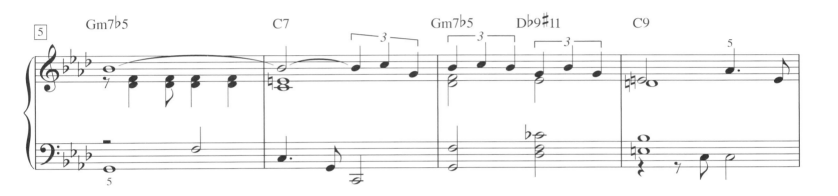

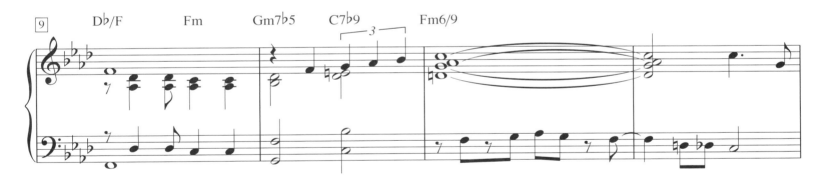

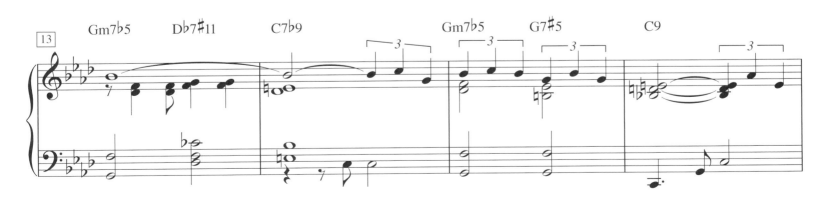

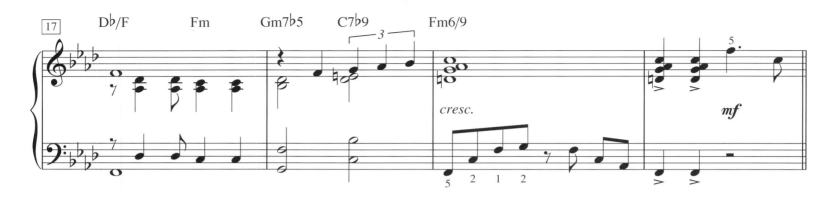

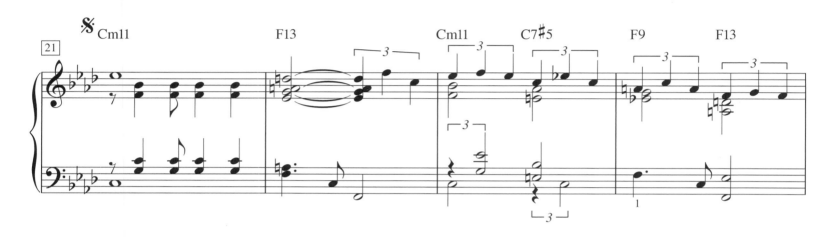

To Coda ⊕

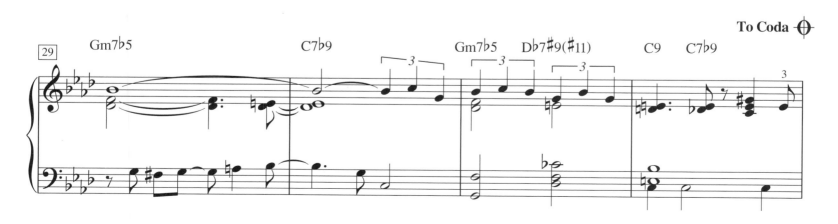

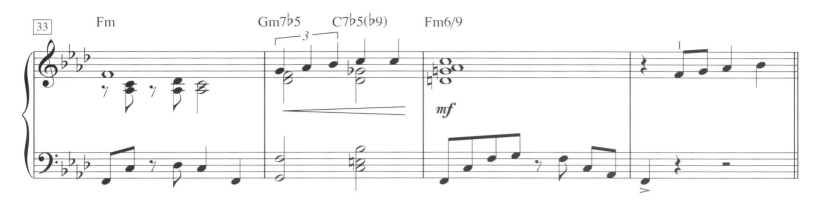

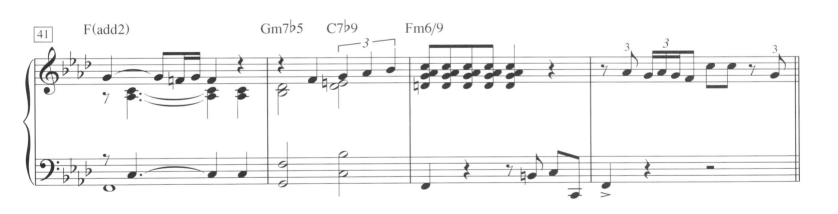

BLUES FOR MARTHA

By OSCAR PETERSON

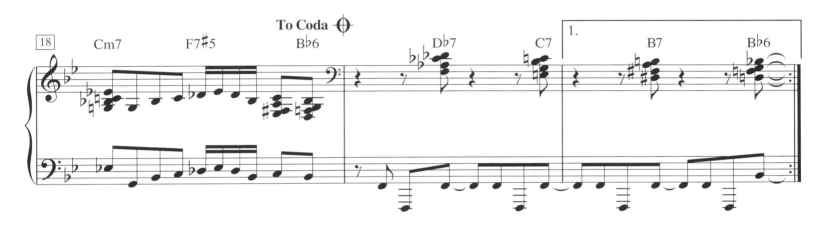

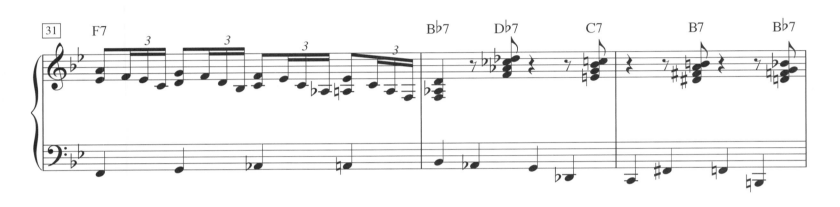

BLUES IN A MINOR

By JOHN LEWIS

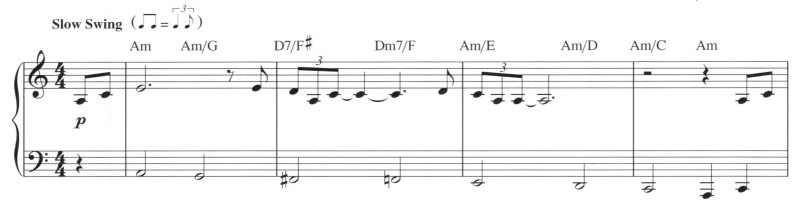

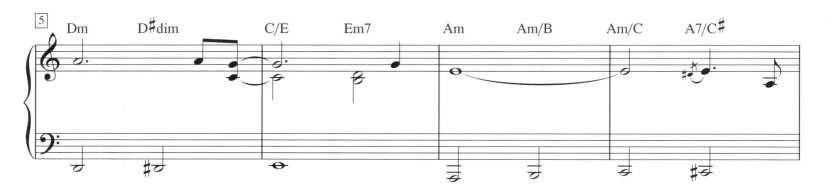

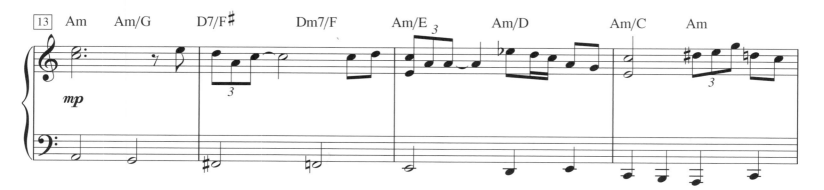

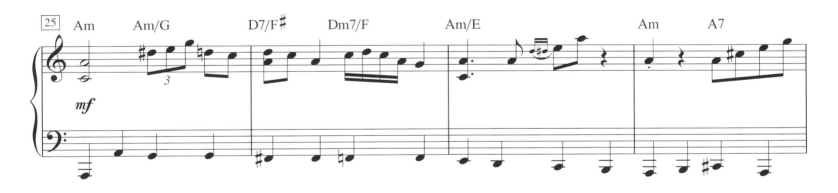

BLUES IN THE CLOSET

By OSCAR PETTIFORD

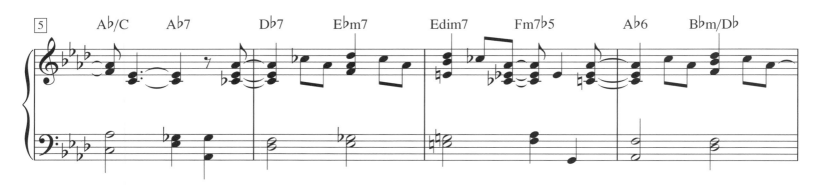

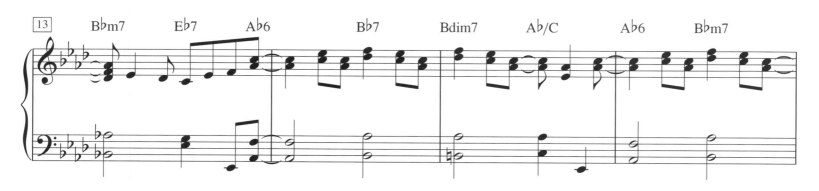

BORN TO BE BLUE

Words by ROBERT WELLS
Music by MEL TORMÉ

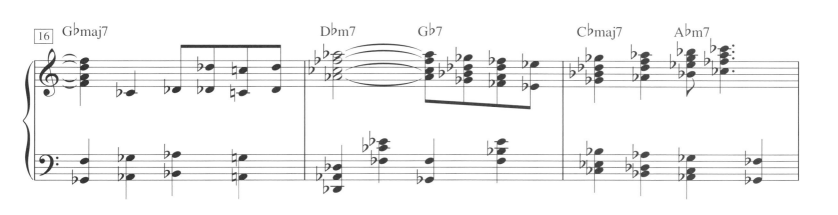

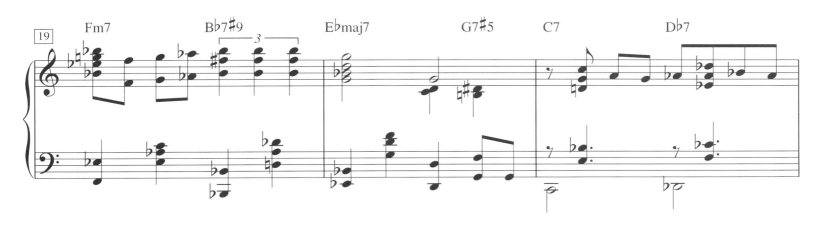

BOUNCING WITH BUD

Words and Music by EARL "BUD" POWELL
and WALTER GIL FULLER

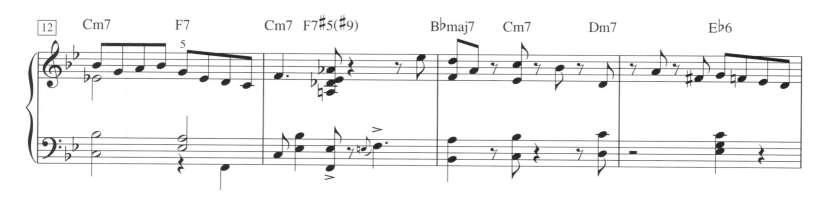

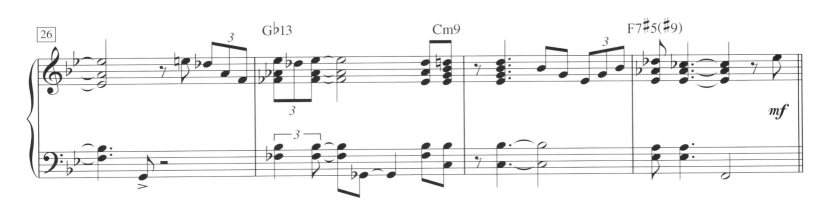

72

BREMOND'S BLUES

By CEDAR WALTON

C-JAM BLUES

By DUKE ELLINGTON

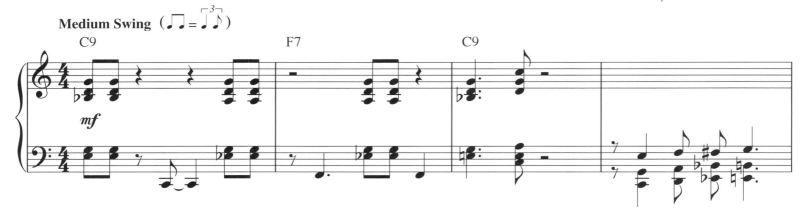

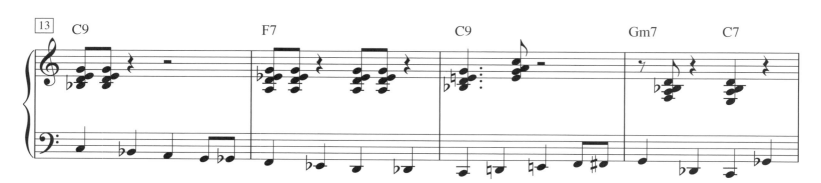

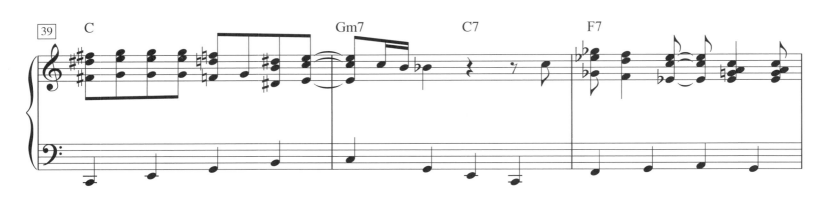

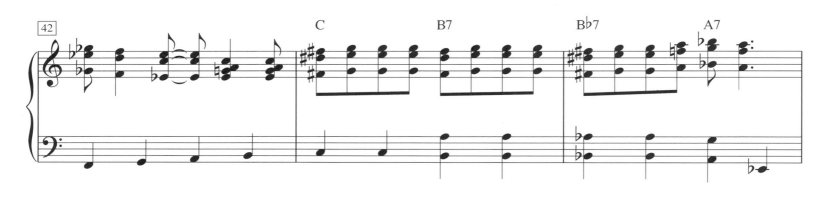

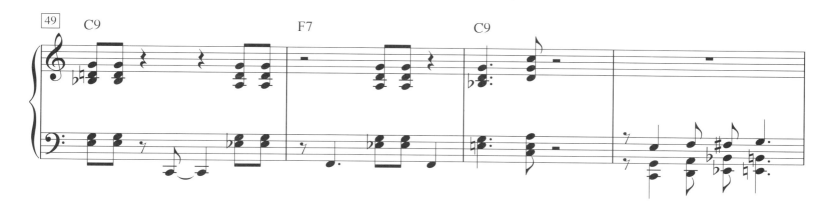

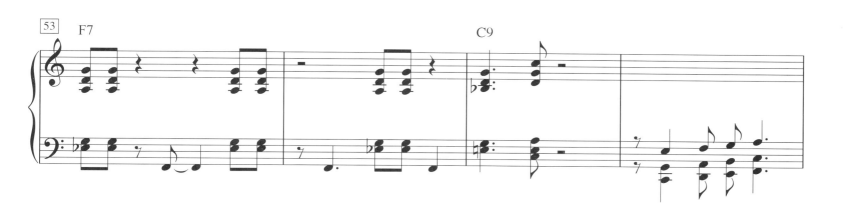

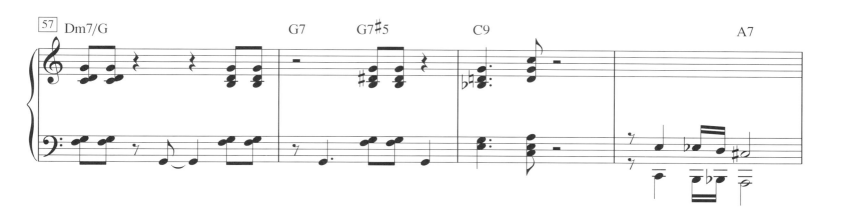

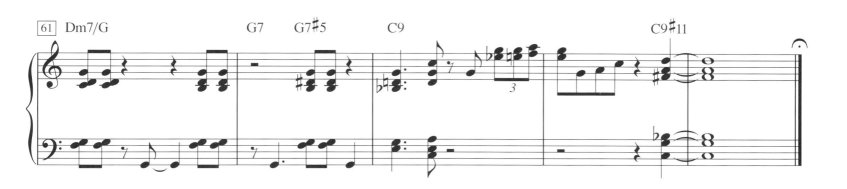

COME SUNDAY
from BLACK, BROWN & BEIGE

By DUKE ELLINGTON

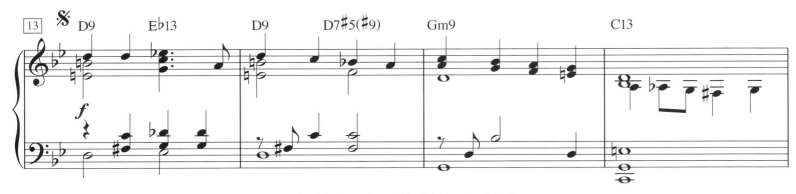

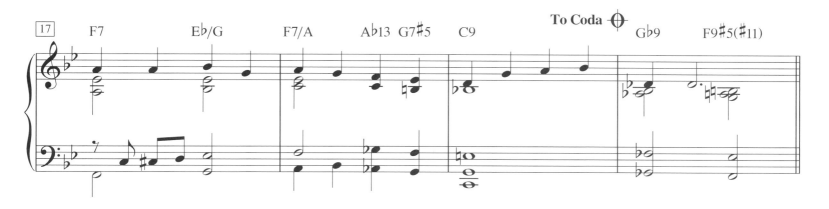

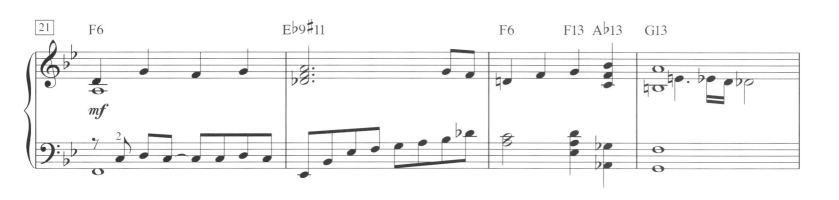

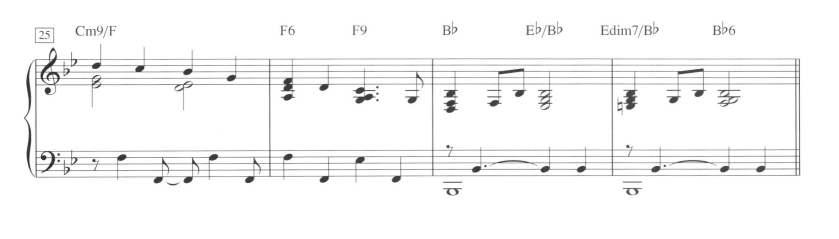

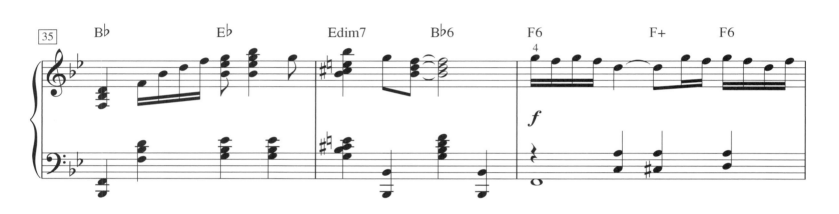

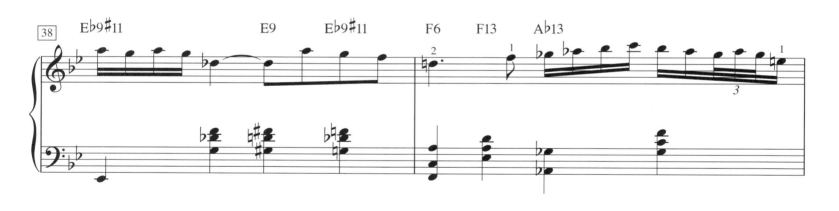

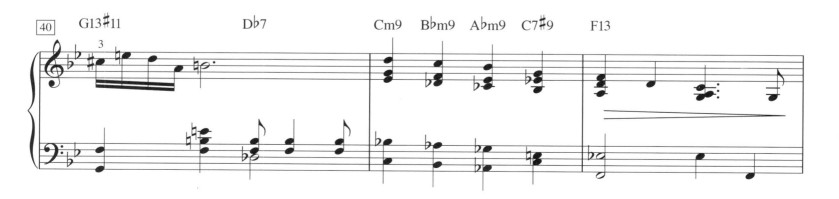

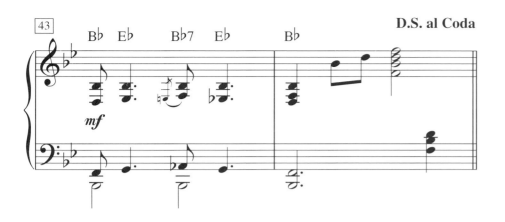

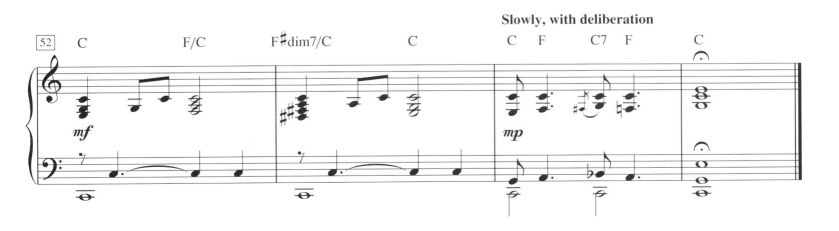

COTTON TAIL

By DUKE ELLINGTON

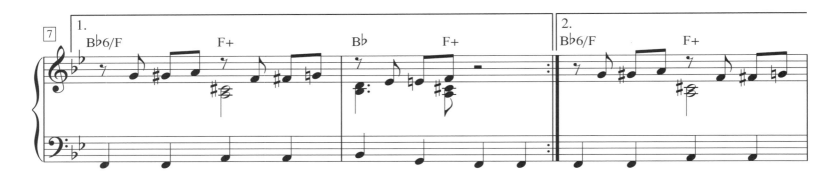

CRAZEOLOGY

By BENNIE HARRIS

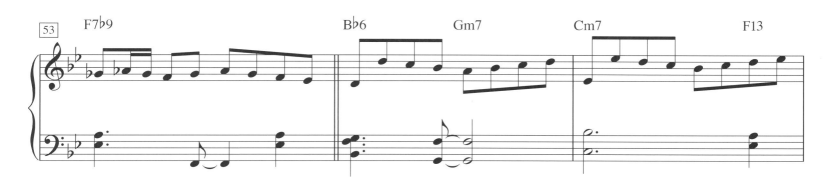

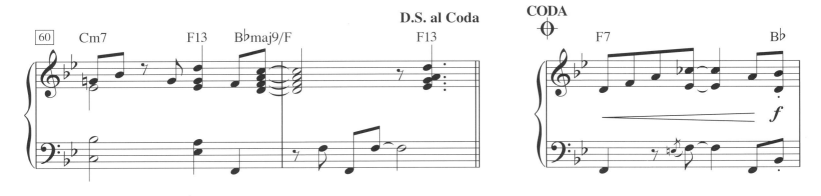

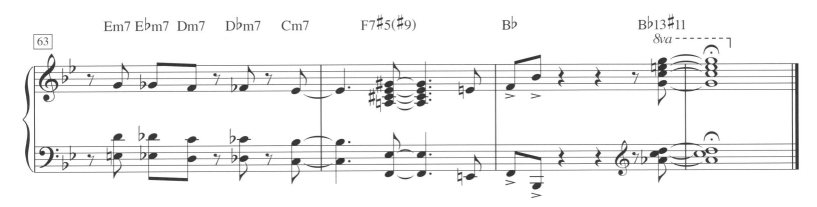

DAY DREAM

By DUKE ELLINGTON
and BILLY STRAYHORN

Slow Ballad

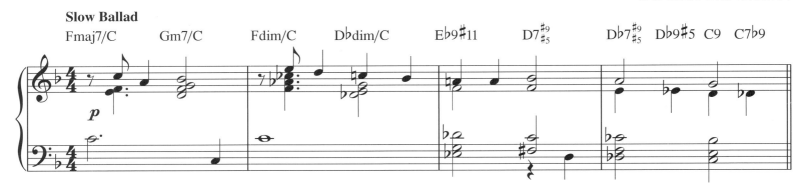

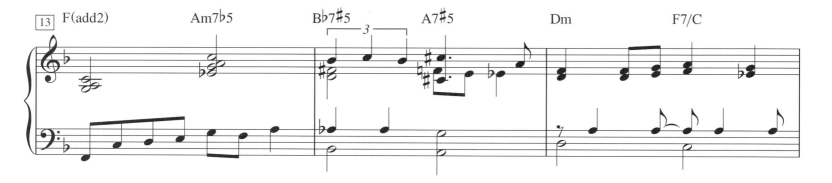

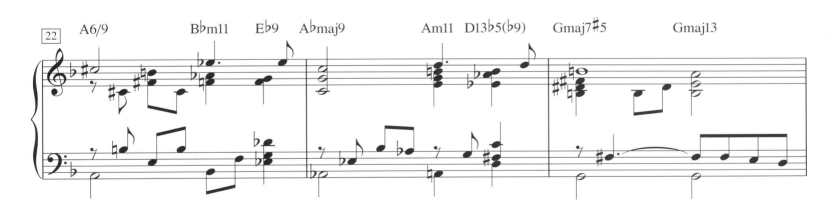

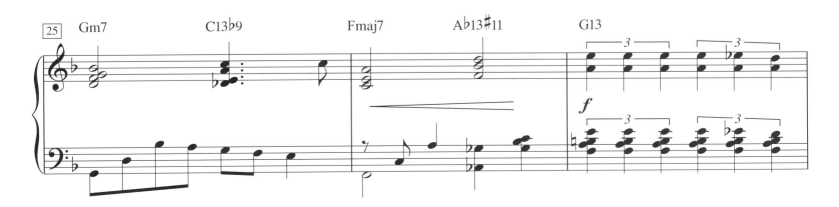

94

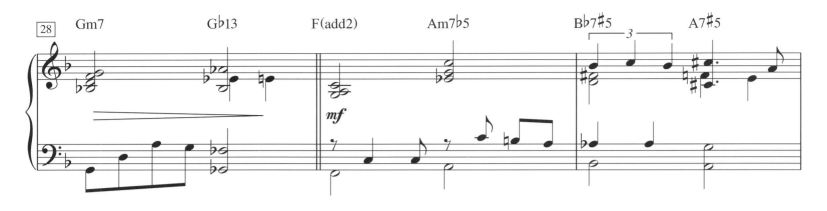

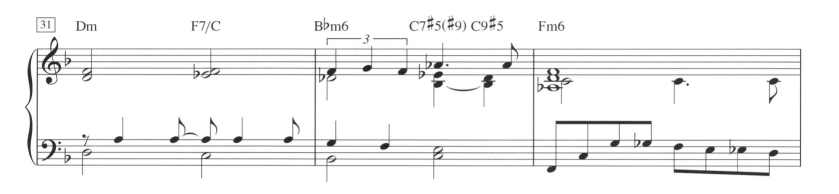

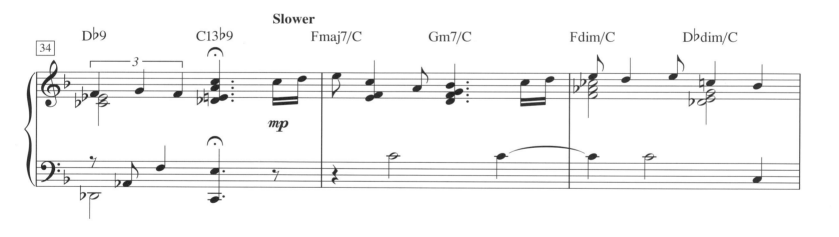

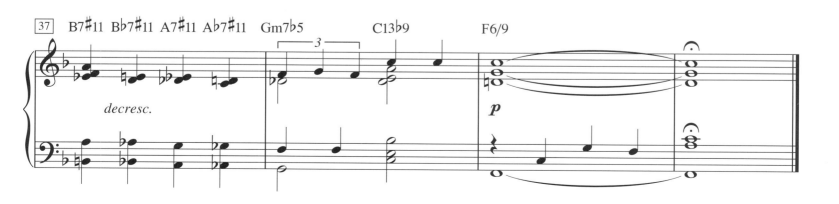

DOODLIN'

By HORACE SILVER

DEAR OLD STOCKHOLM

Swedish Folk Song

99

DELAUNEY'S DILEMMA

By JOHN LEWIS

104

DJANGO

By JOHN LEWIS

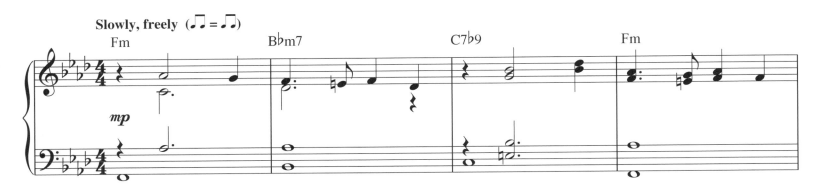

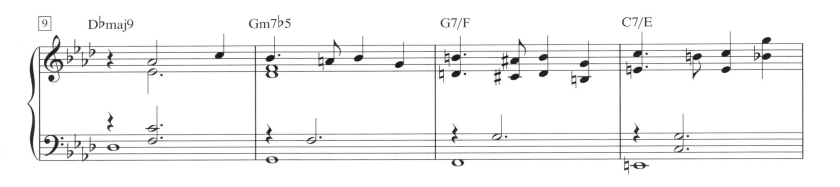

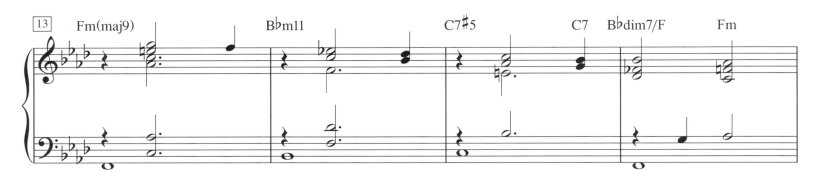

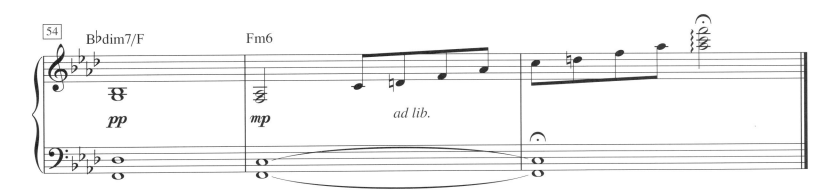

DOLPHIN DANCE

By HERBIE HANCOCK

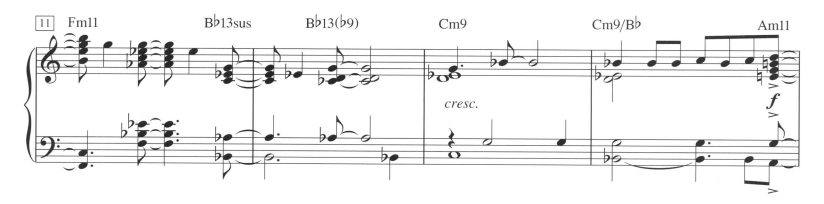

112

DON'T YOU KNOW I CARE
(Or Don't You Care to Know)

Words by MACK DAVID
Music by DUKE ELLINGTON

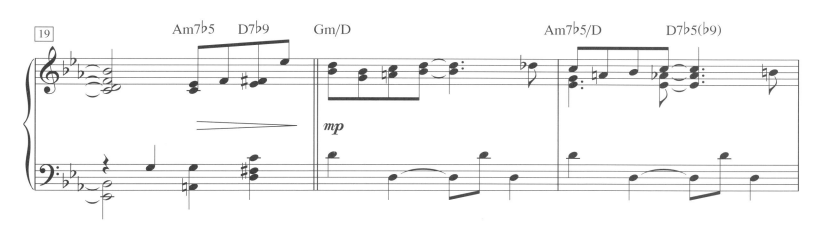

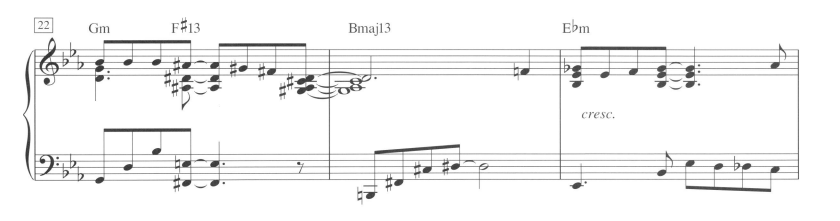

116

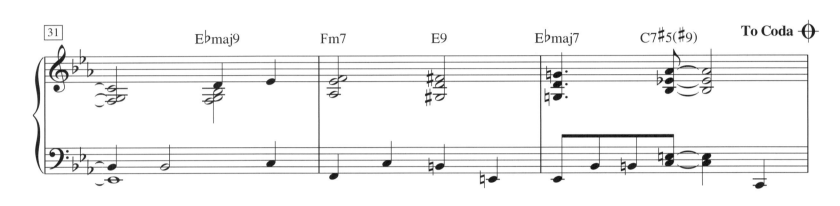

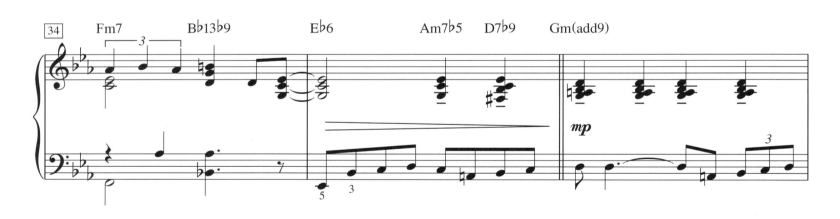

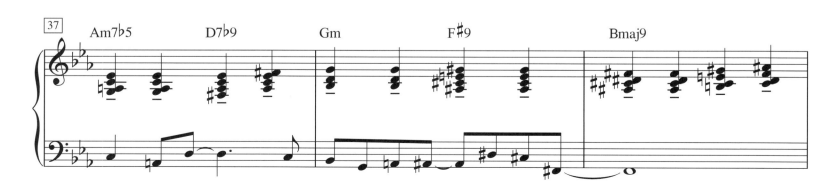

117

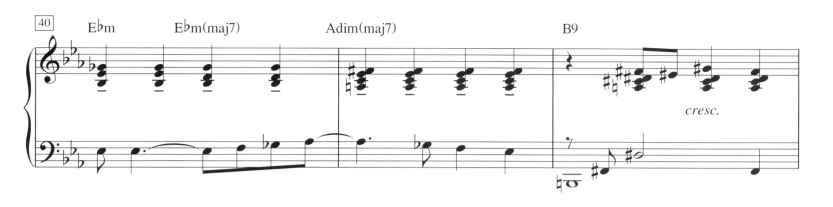

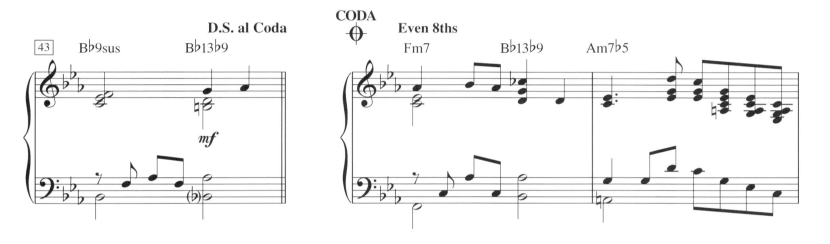

DOXY

By SONNY ROLLINS

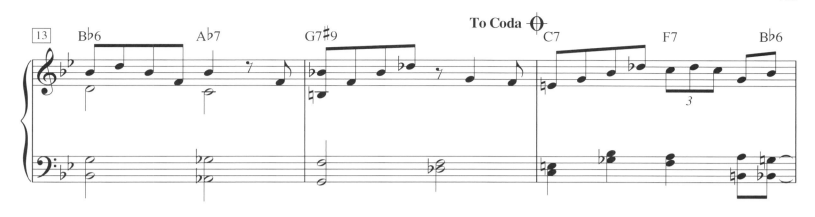

EVERYTHING BUT YOU

By DUKE ELLINGTON,
HARRY JAMES and DON GEORGE

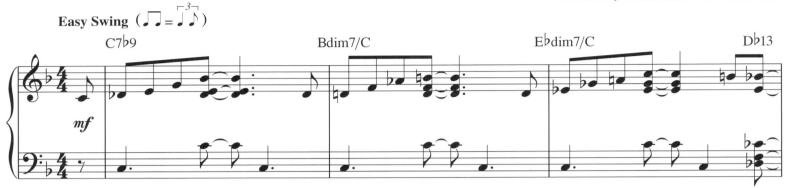

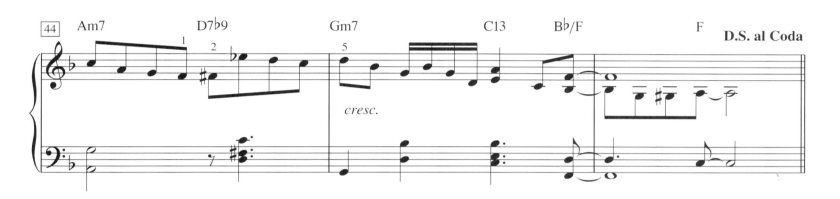

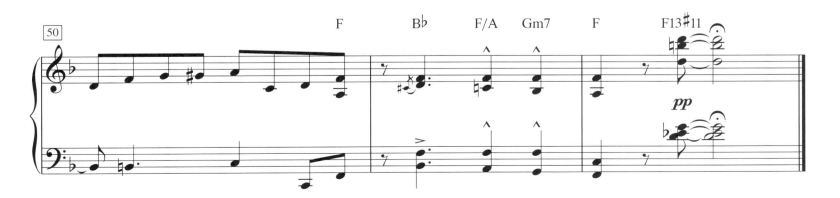

52nd STREET THEME

By THELONIOUS MONK

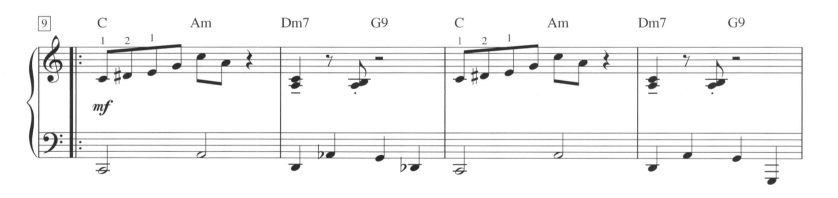

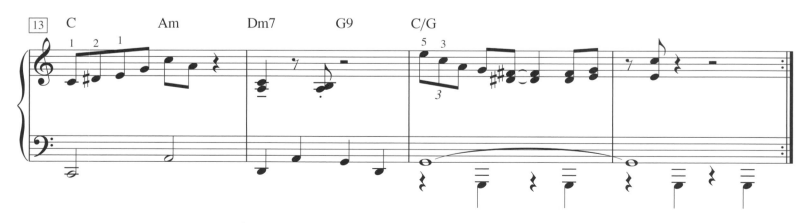

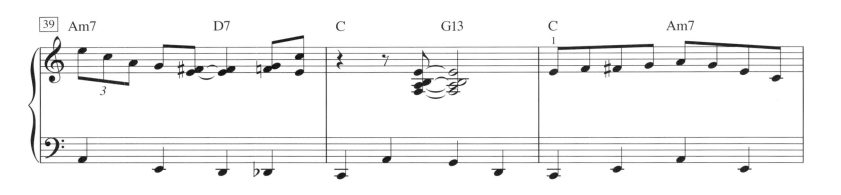

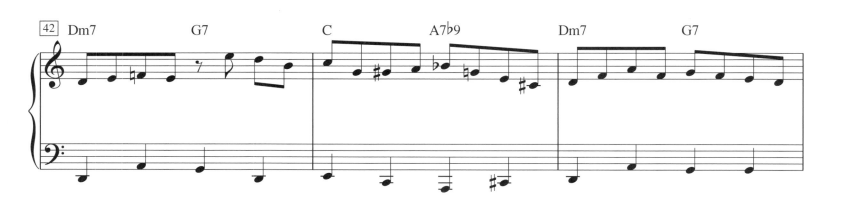

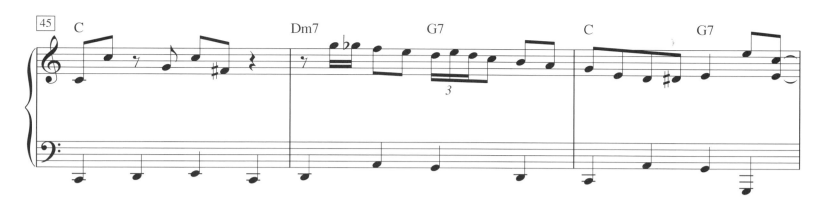

GIANT STEPS

By JOHN COLTRANE

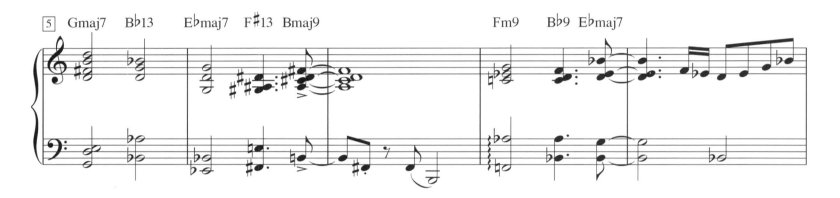

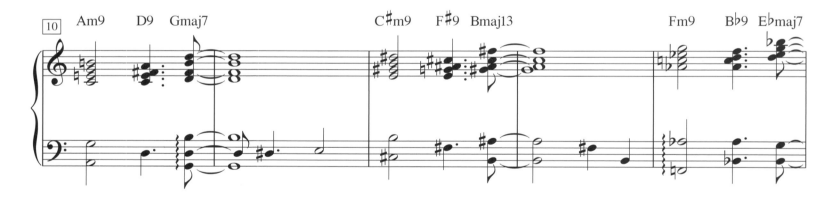

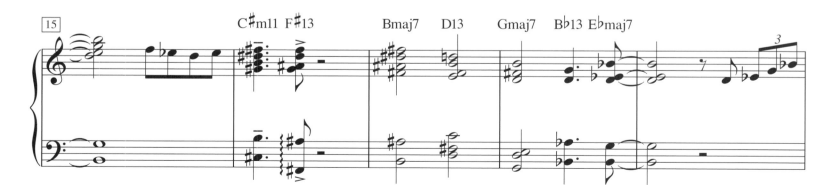

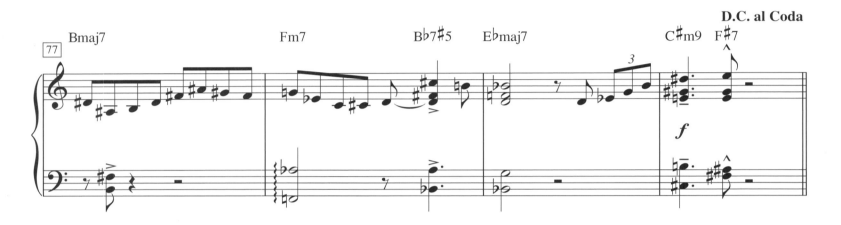

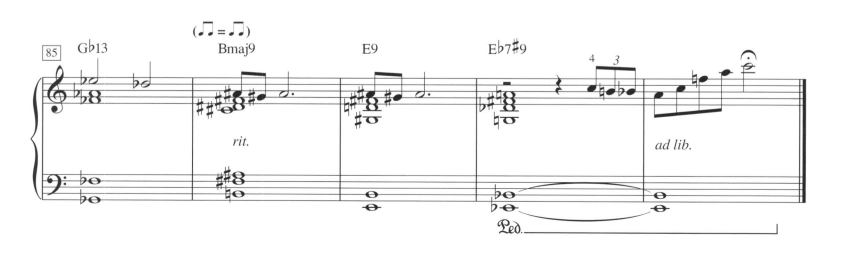

THE GOLDEN STRIKER

By JOHN LEWIS

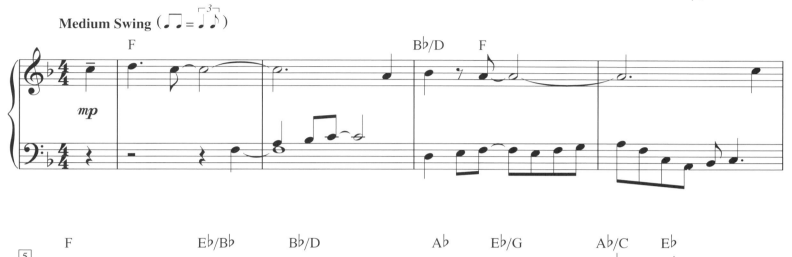

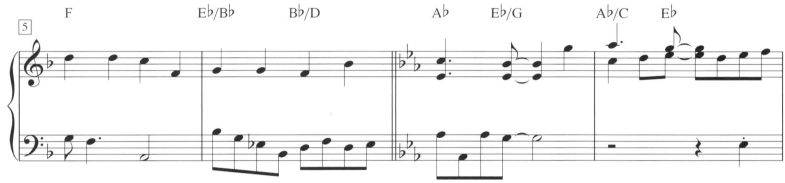

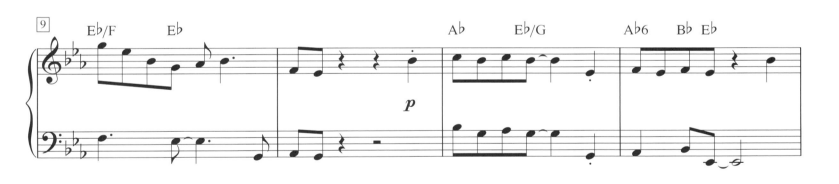

To Coda

GINGER BREAD BOY

By JIMMY HEATH

GOTTA BE THIS OR THAT

Words and Music by
SUNNY SKYLAR

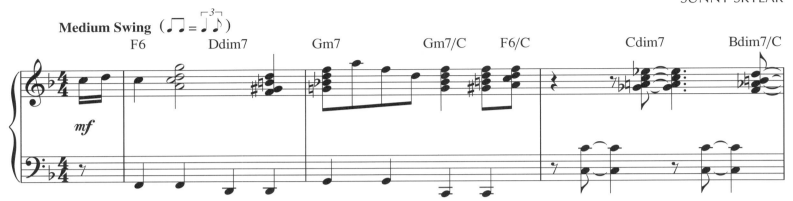

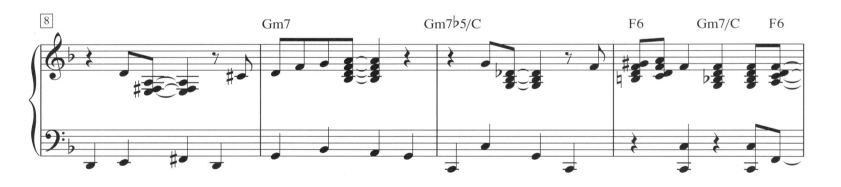

GRAVY WALTZ

Lyrics by STEVE ALLEN
Music by RAY BROWN

*First chorus based on one by Oscar Peterson.

149

151

GROOVIN' HIGH

By JOHN "DIZZY" GILLESPIE

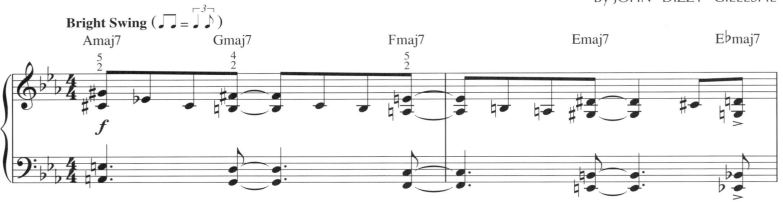

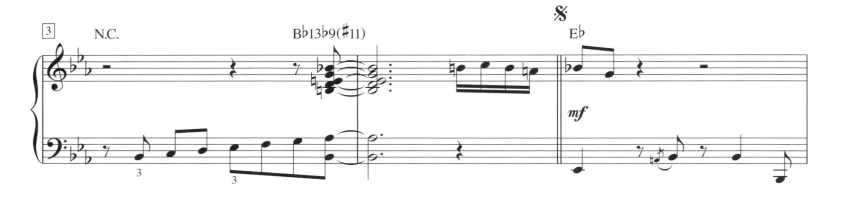

154

155

IN WALKED BUD

By THELONIOUS MONK

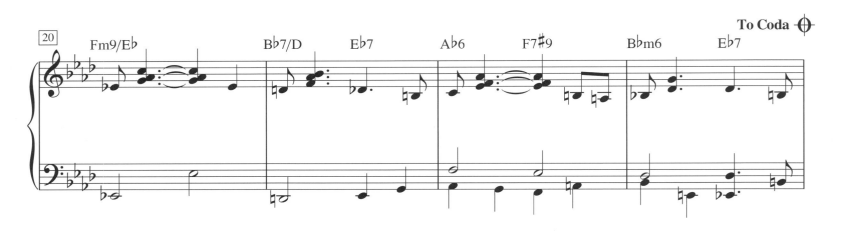

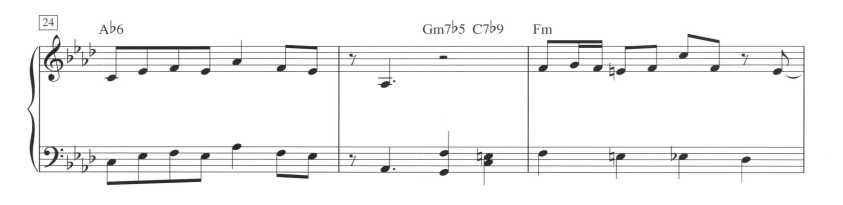

159

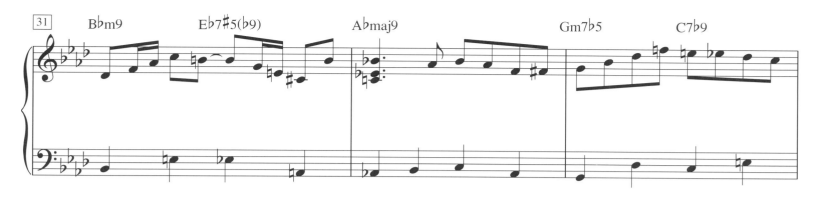

I HEAR A RHAPSODY

By GEORGE FRAJOS,
JACK BAKER and DICK GASPARRE

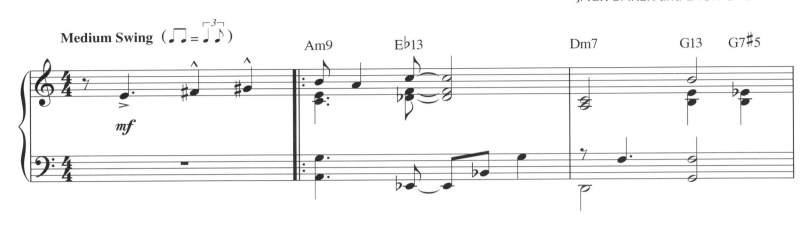

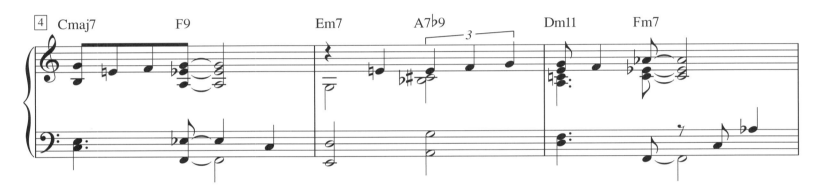

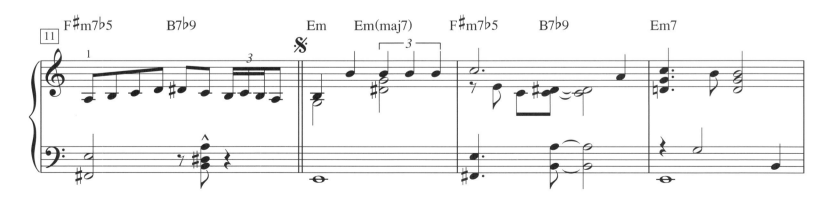

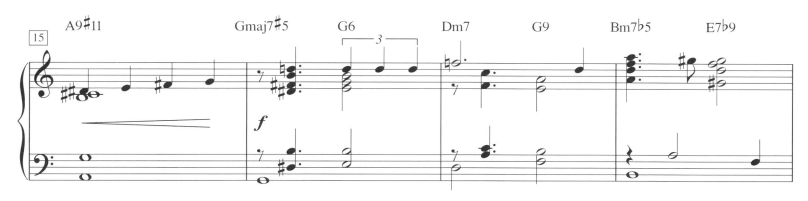

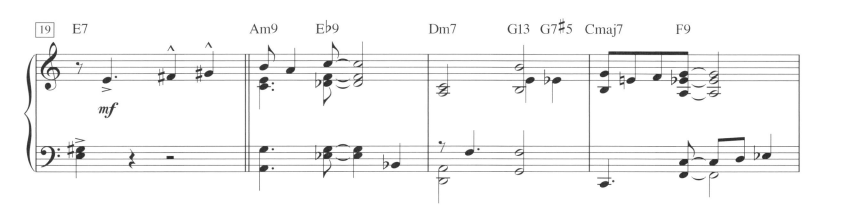

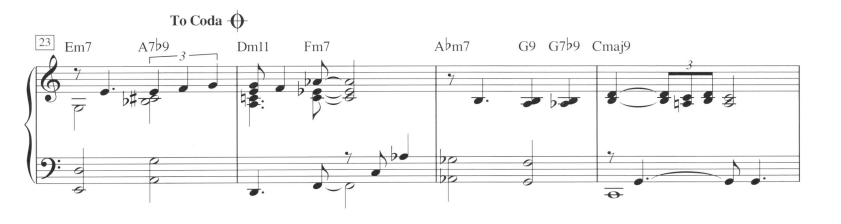

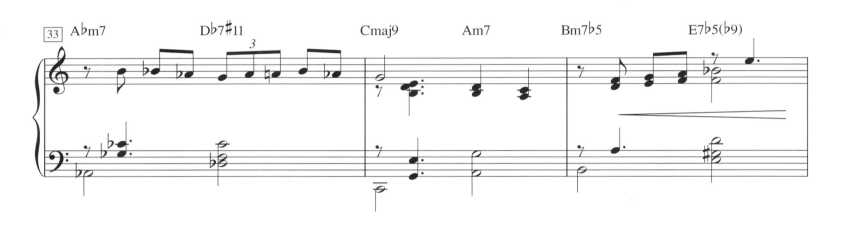

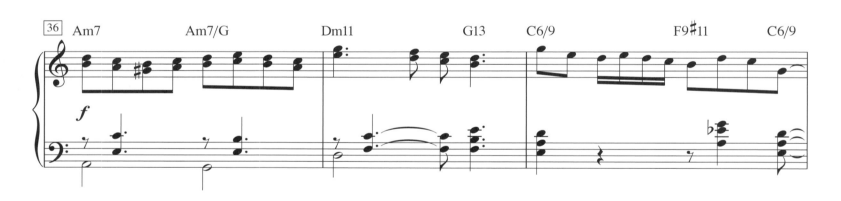

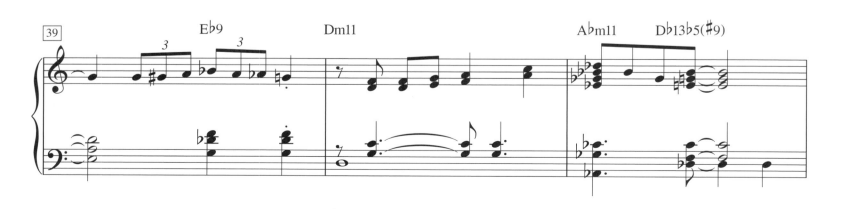

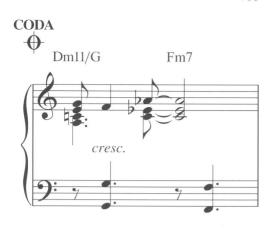

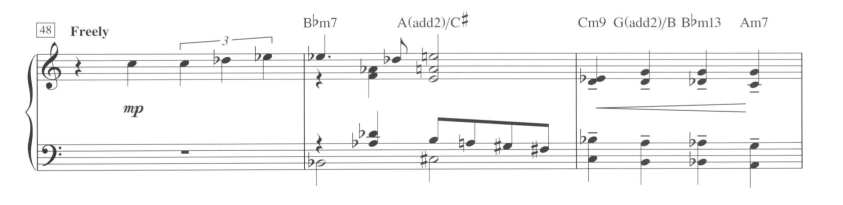

I MEAN YOU

By THELONIOUS MONK
and COLEMAN HAWKINS

INTERMEZZO

By HEINZ PROVOST
and ROBERT HENNING

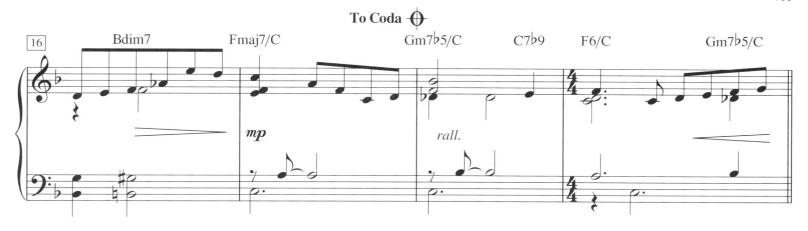

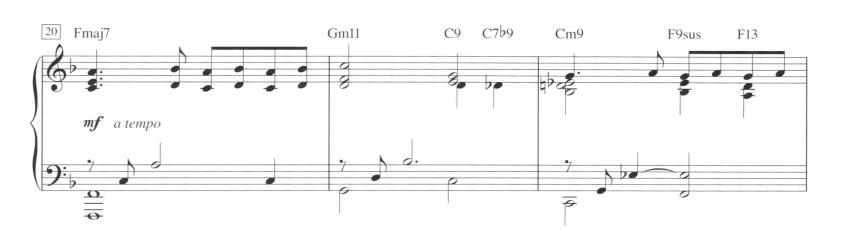

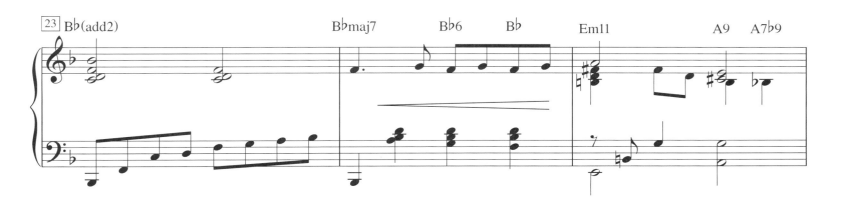

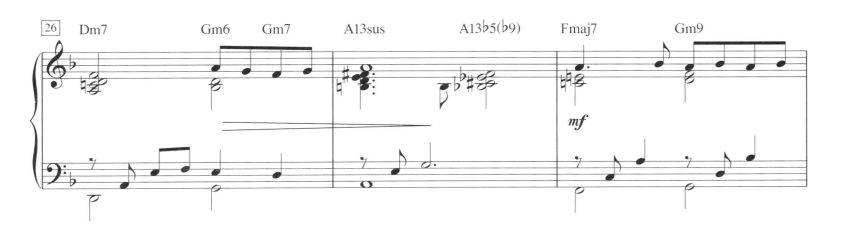

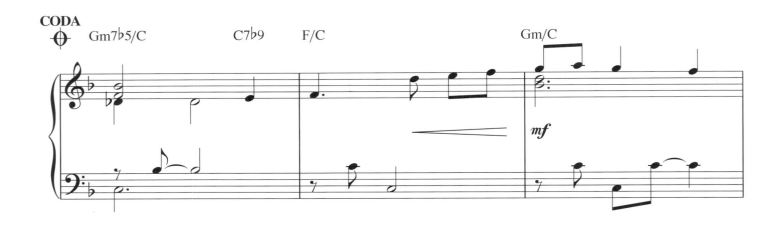

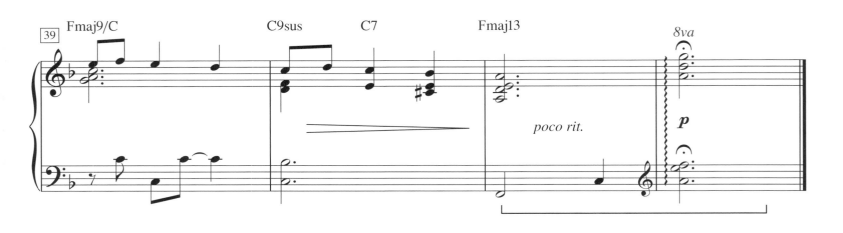

KILLER JOE

By BENNY GOLSON

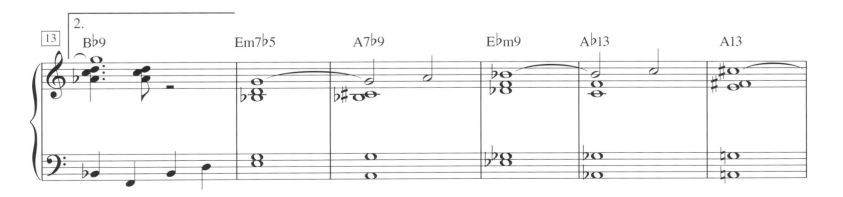

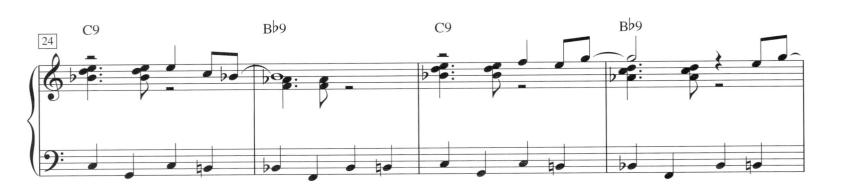

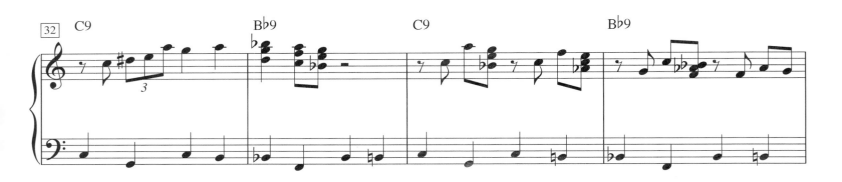

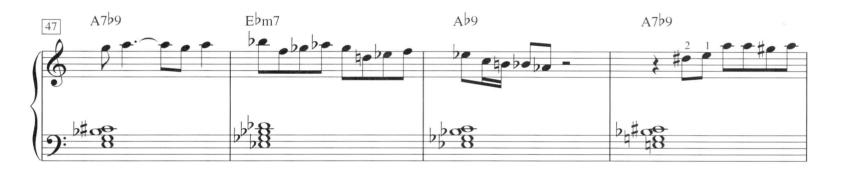

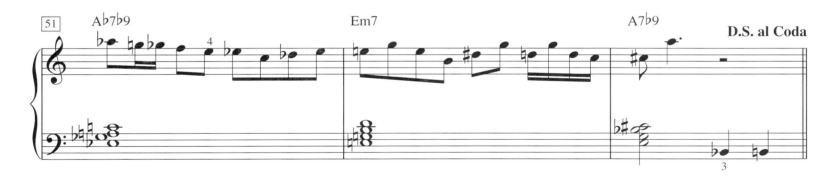

INVITATION

Words by PAUL FRANCIS WEBSTER
Music by BRONISLAU KAPER

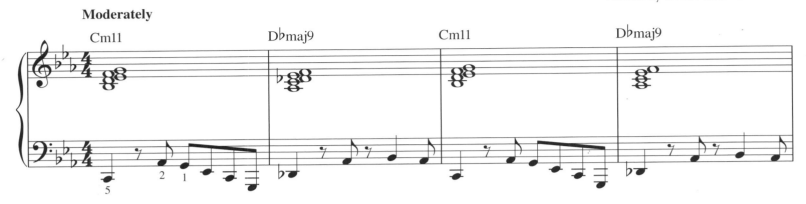

175

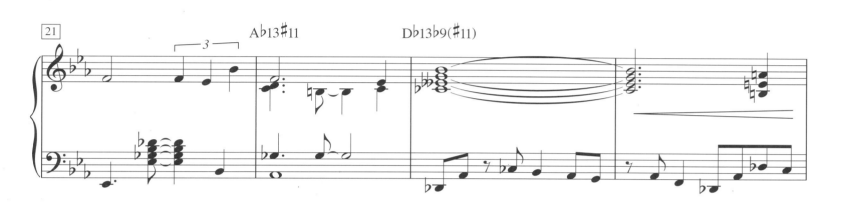

JERU

By GERRY MULLIGAN

JORDU

By DUKE JORDAN

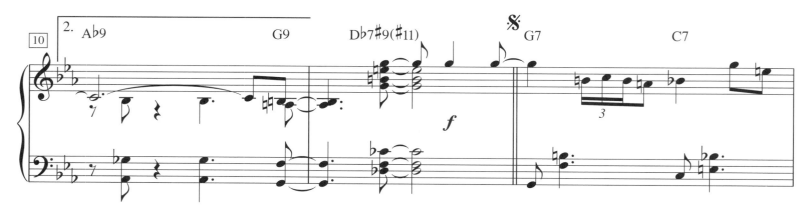

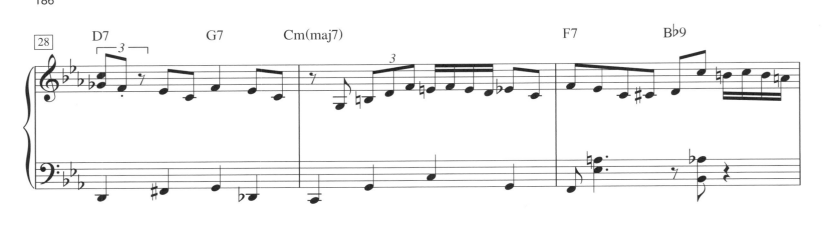

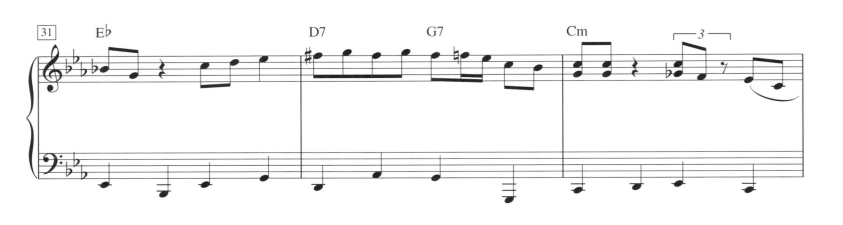

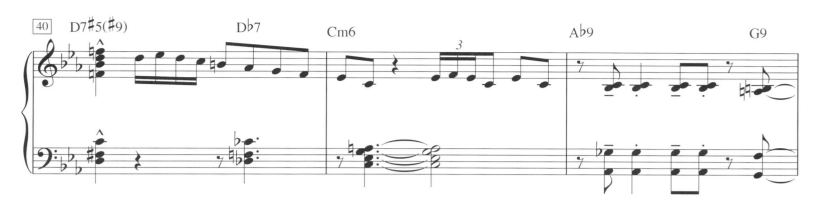

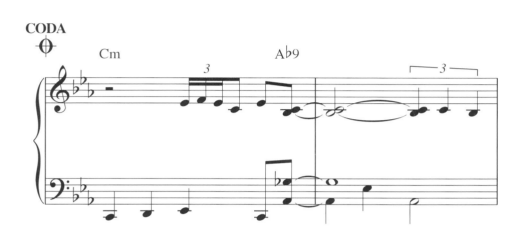

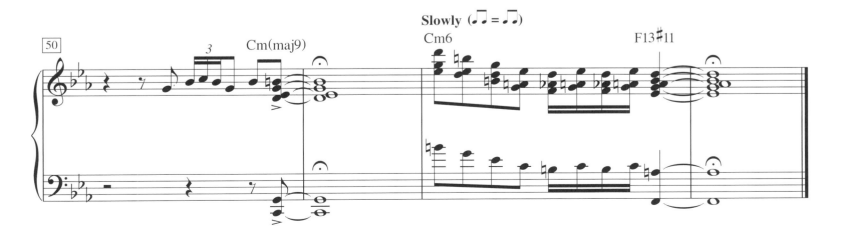

LIKE YOUNG

Words and Music by PAUL WEBSTER
and ANDRÉ PREVIN

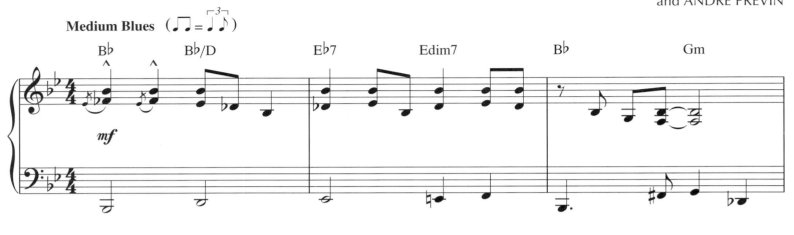

189

190

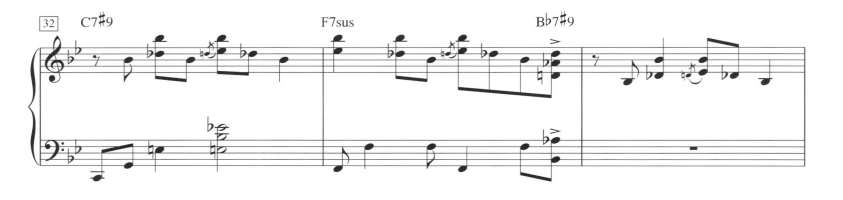

MY LITTLE SUEDE SHOES

By CHARLIE PARKER

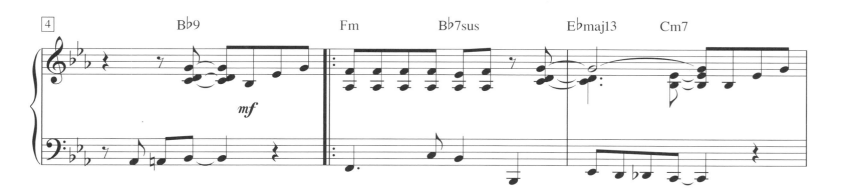

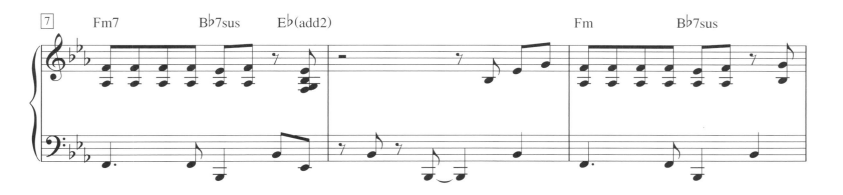

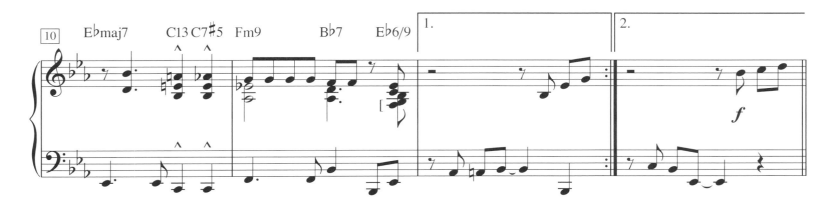

193

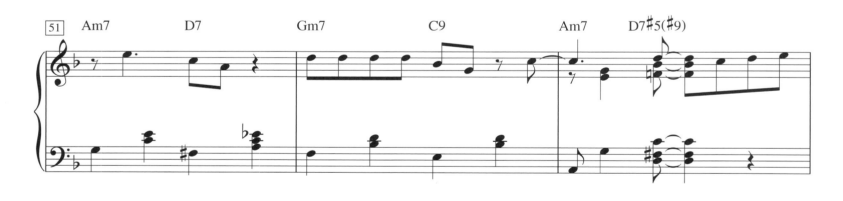

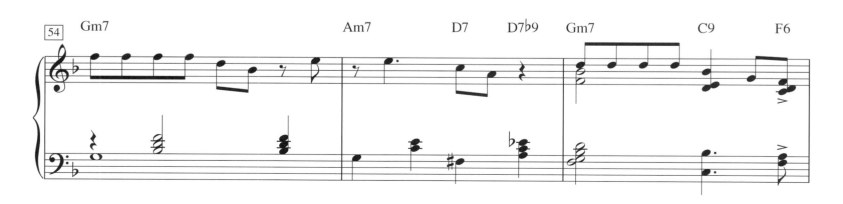

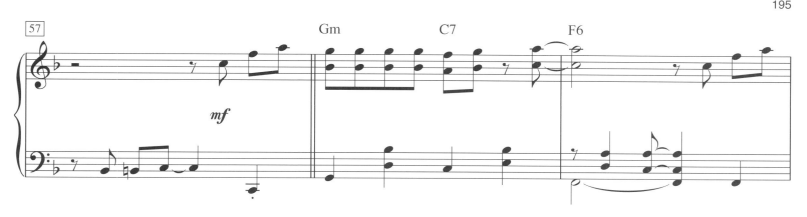

LINE FOR LYONS

By GERRY MULLIGAN

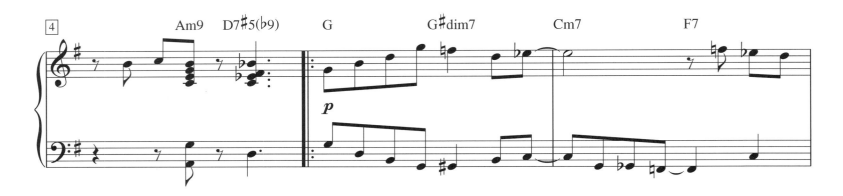

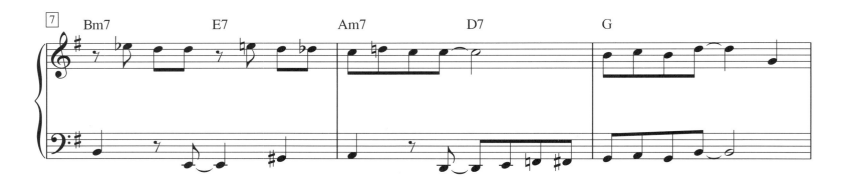

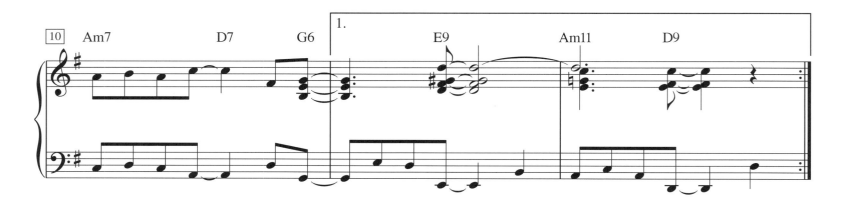

198

Adapted from Gerry Mulligan's solo on "King of Cool Jazz"

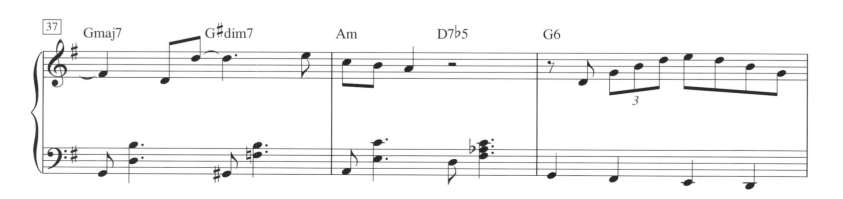

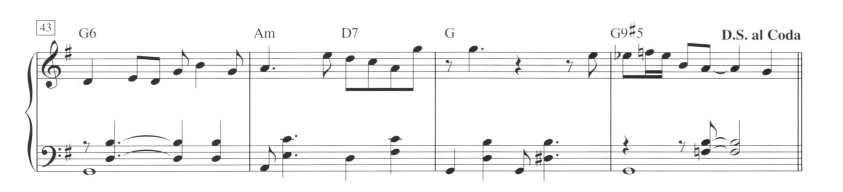

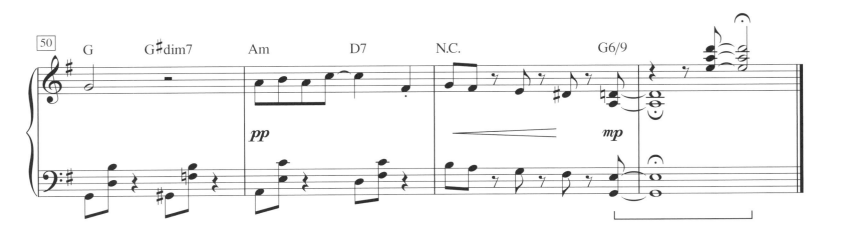

MIDNIGHT SUN

Words and Music by LIONEL HAMPTON,
SONNY BURKE and JOHNNY MERCER

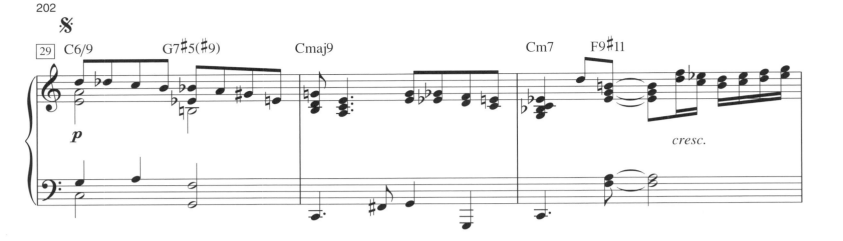

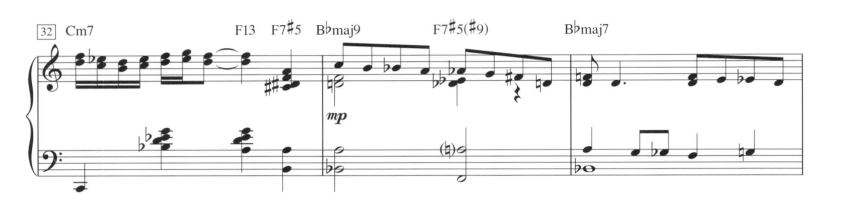

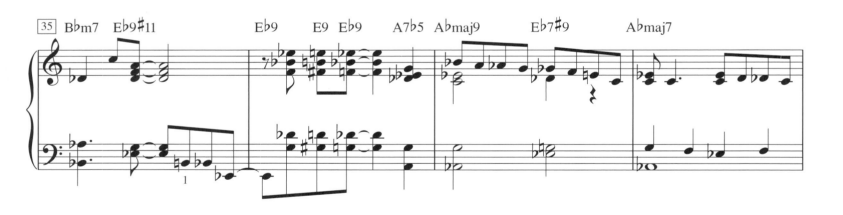

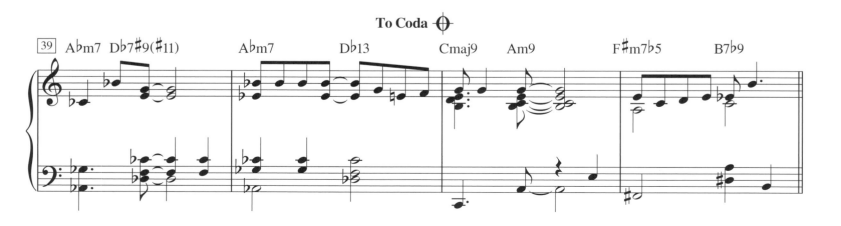

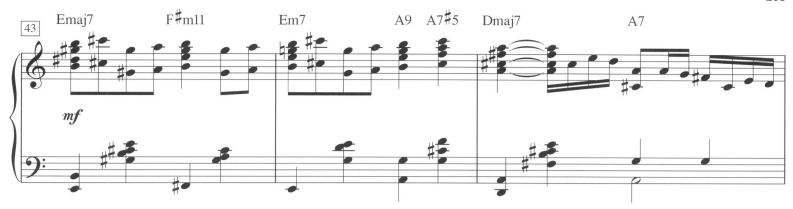

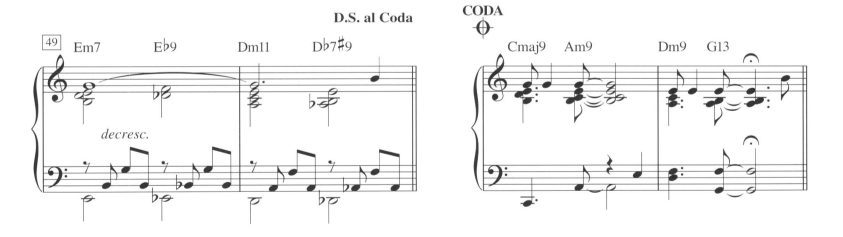

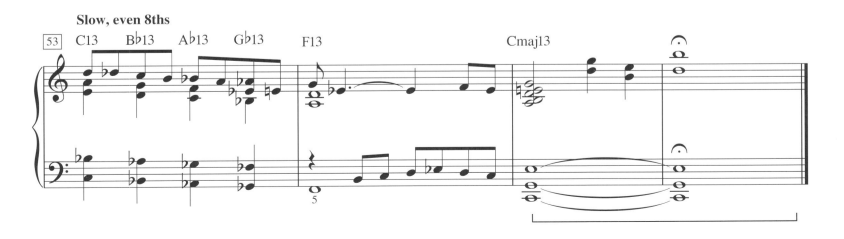

MOONLIGHT IN VERMONT

Words by JOHN BLACKBURN
Music by KARL SUESSDORF

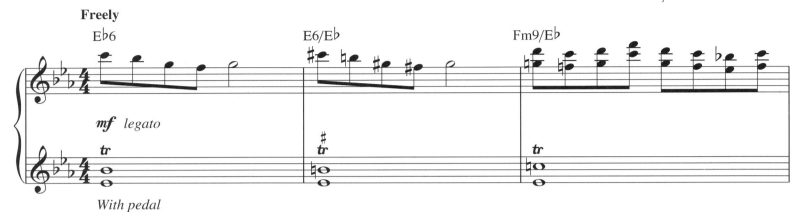

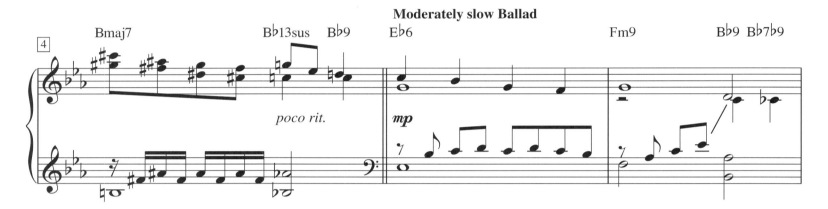

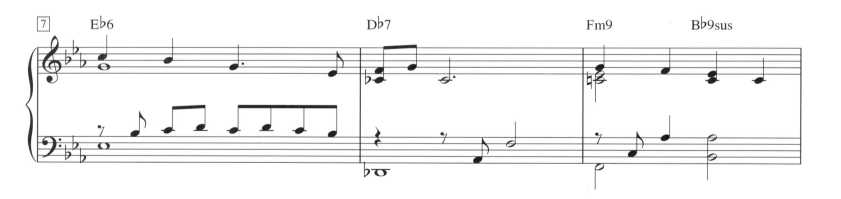

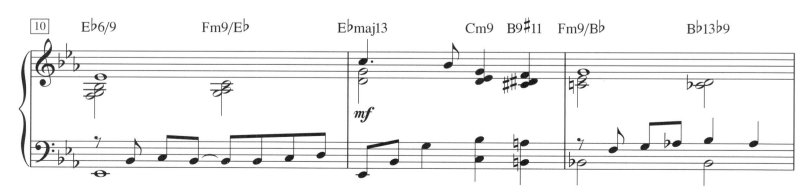

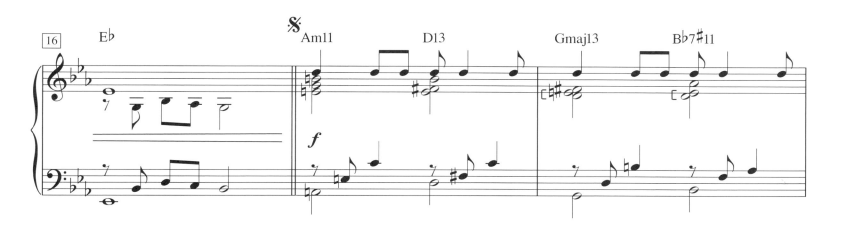

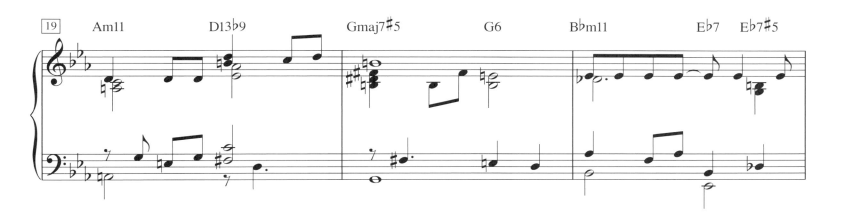

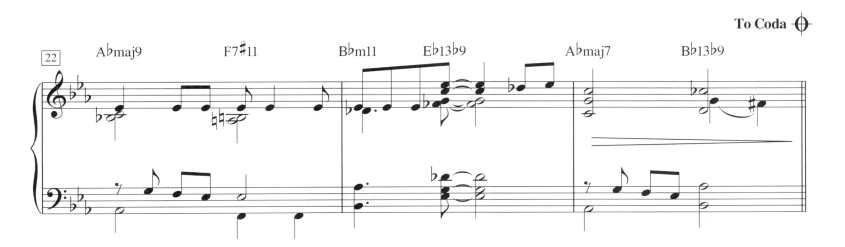

MOTEN SWING

By BUSTER MOTEN
and BENNIE MOTEN

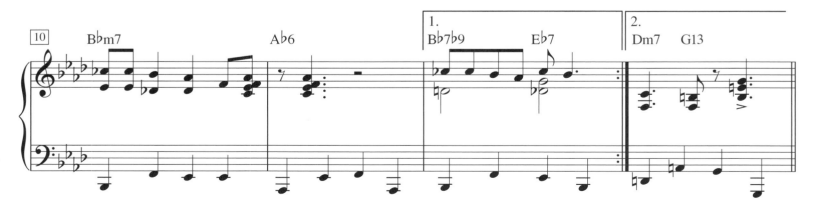

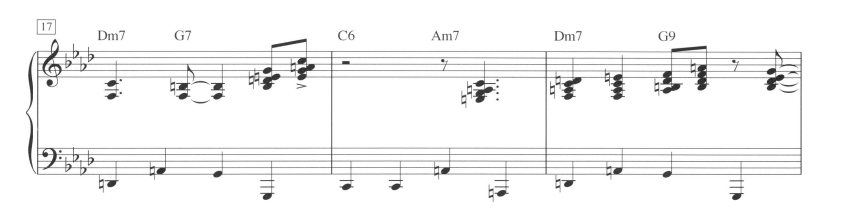

To Coda ⊕

D.S. al Coda

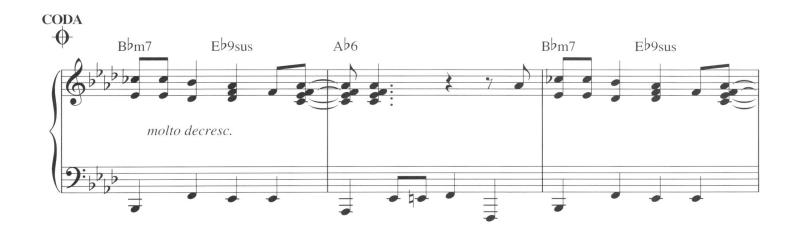

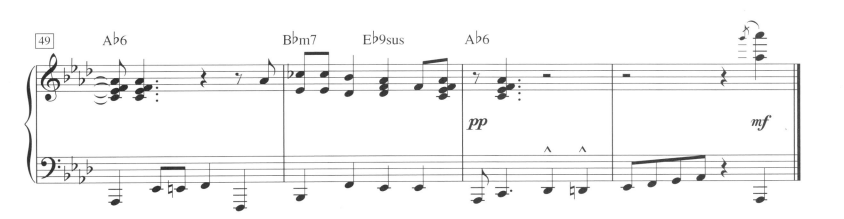

NICA'S DREAM

Words and Music by
HORACE SILVER

Moderately fast Latin

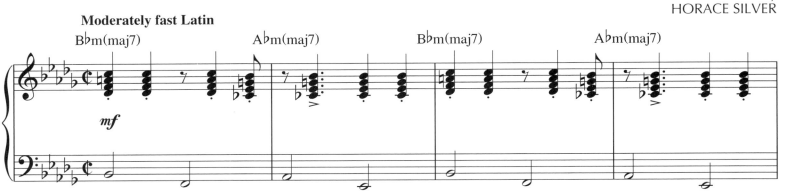

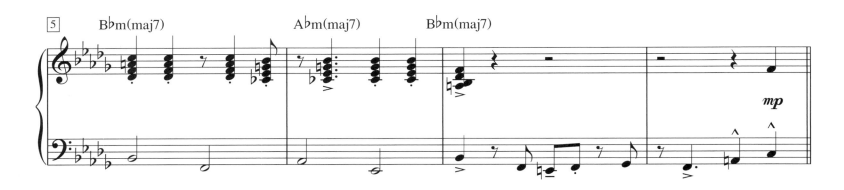

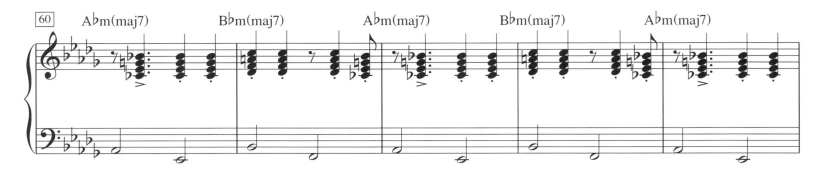

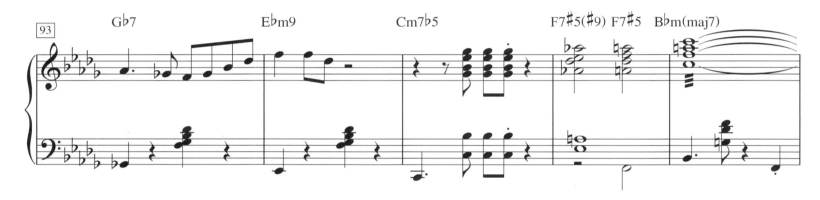

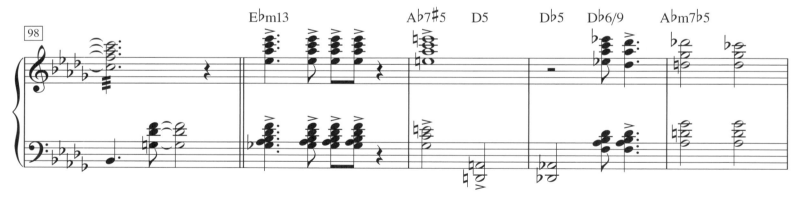

A NIGHT IN TUNISIA

By JOHN "DIZZY" GILLESPIE
and FRANK PAPARELLI

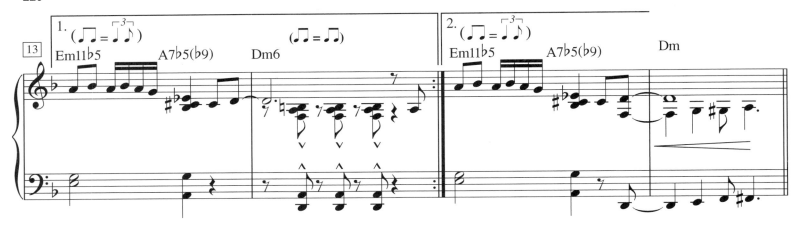

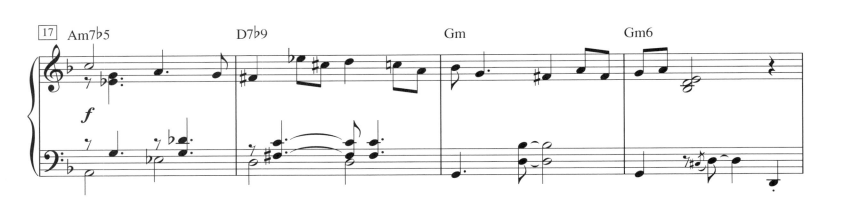

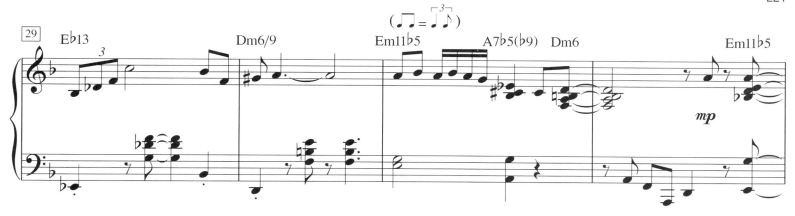

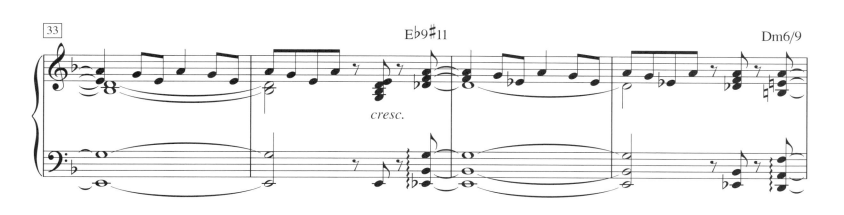

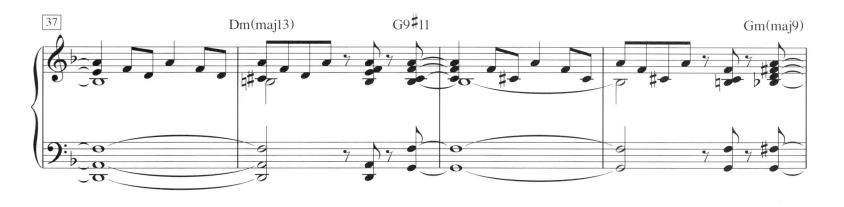

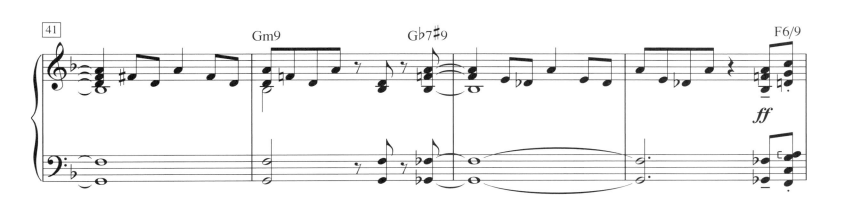

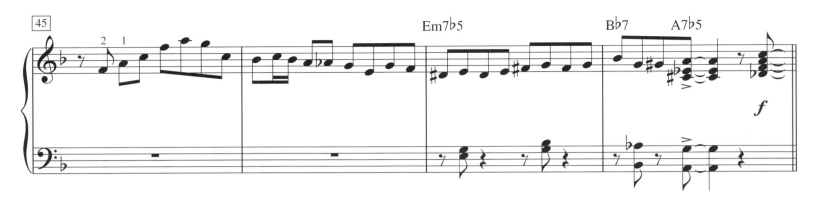

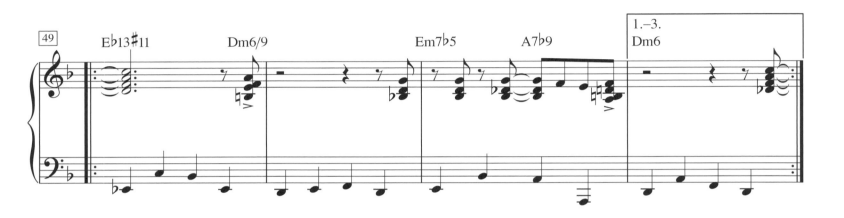

223

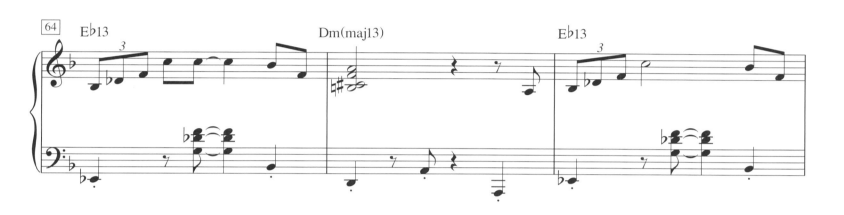

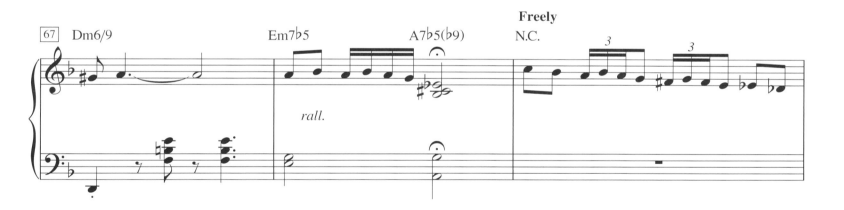

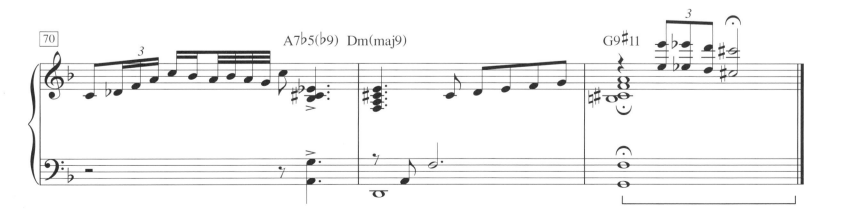

NIGHT TRAIN

Words by OSCAR WASHINGTON and LEWIS C. SIMPKINS
Music by JIMMY FORREST

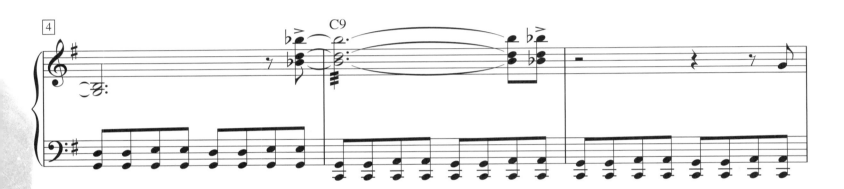

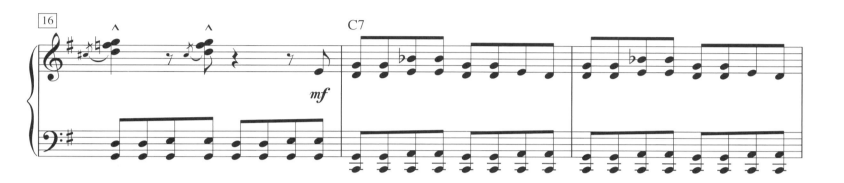

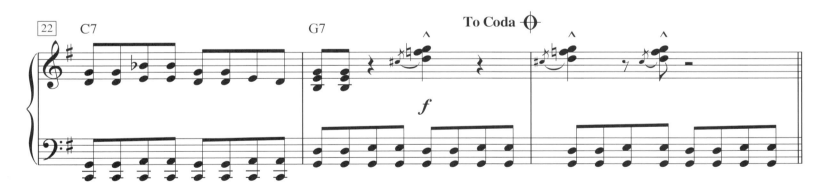

NUAGES

By DJANGO REINHARDT
and JACQUES LARUE

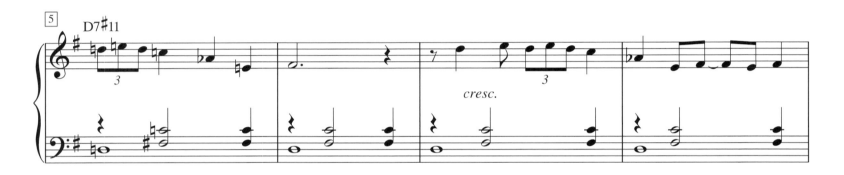

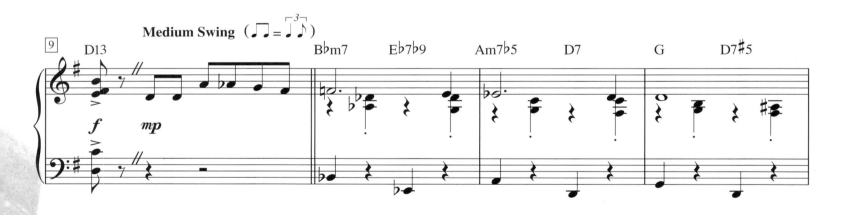

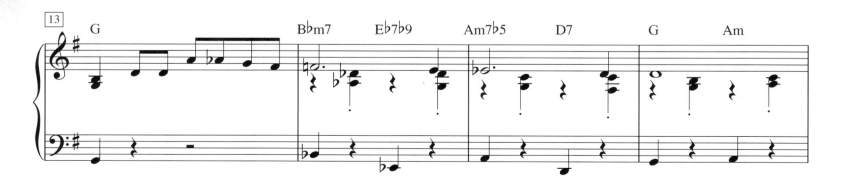

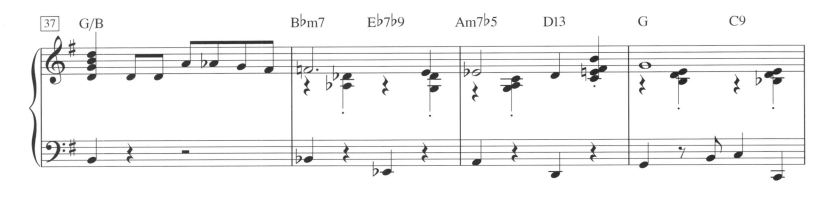

(Adapted from a Django Reinhardt solo)

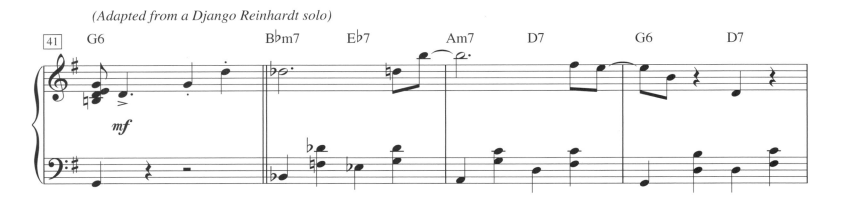

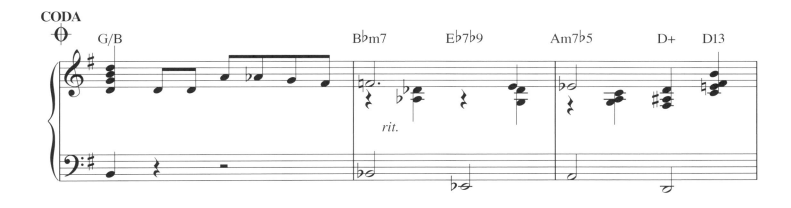

OH, GOOD GRIEF

By VINCE GUARALDI

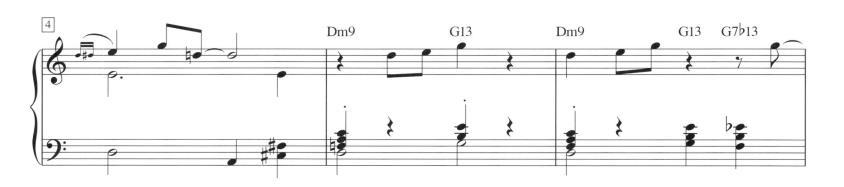

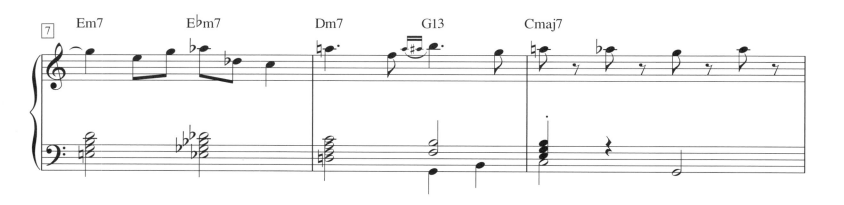

233

234

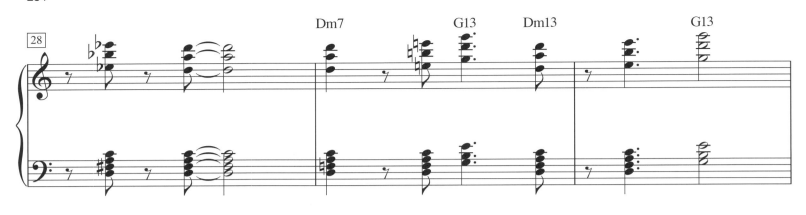

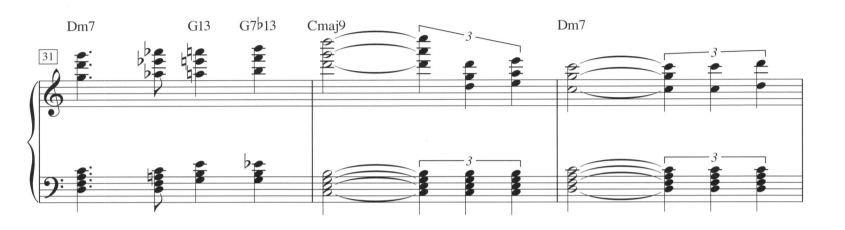

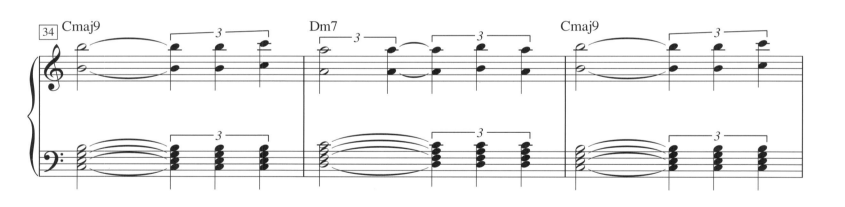

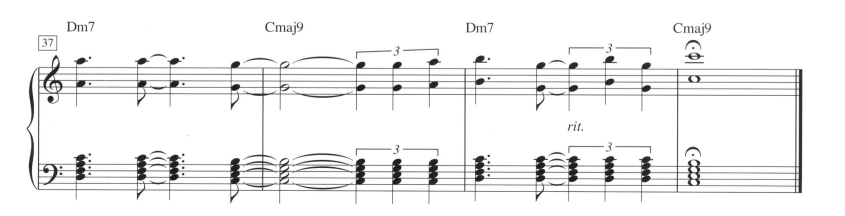

OLEO

By SONNY ROLLINS

ON GREEN DOLPHIN STREET

Lyrics by NED WASHINGTON
Music by BRONISLAU KAPER

240

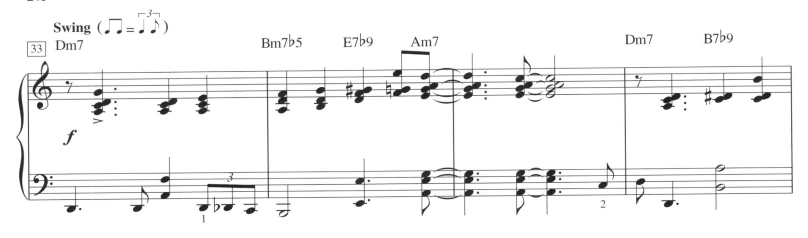

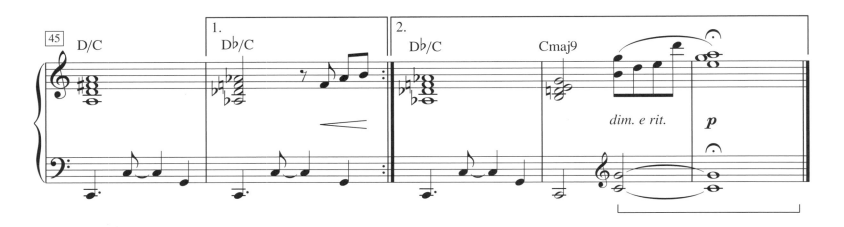

SEVEN COME ELEVEN

By BENNY GOODMAN
and CHARLIE CHRISTIAN

Bright Swing

243

RELAXIN' AT THE CAMARILLO

By CHARLIE PARKER

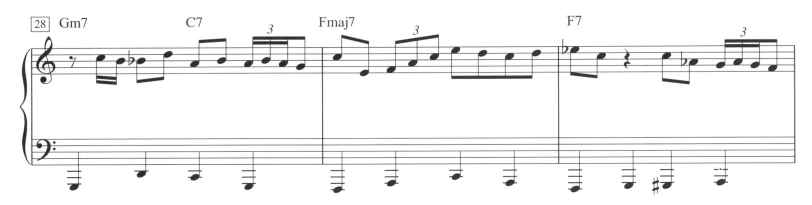

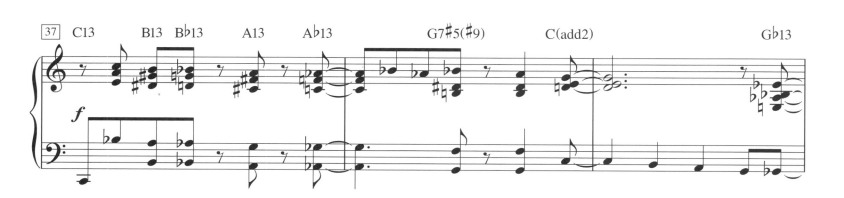

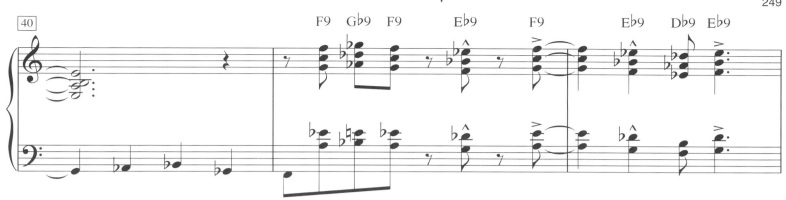

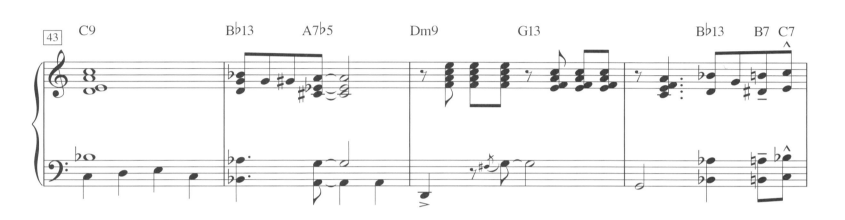

ROBBIN'S NEST

By SIR CHARLES THOMPSON
and ILLINOIS JACQUET

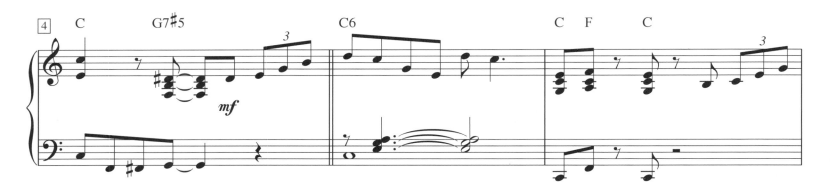

SHINY STOCKINGS

Music by FRANK FOSTER

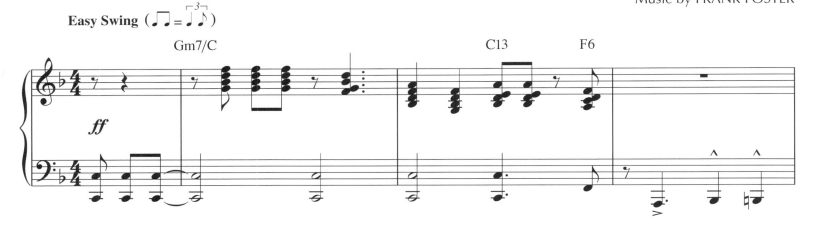

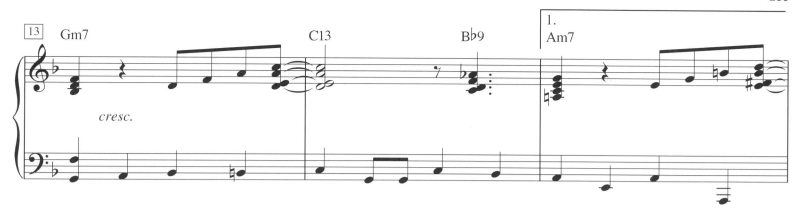

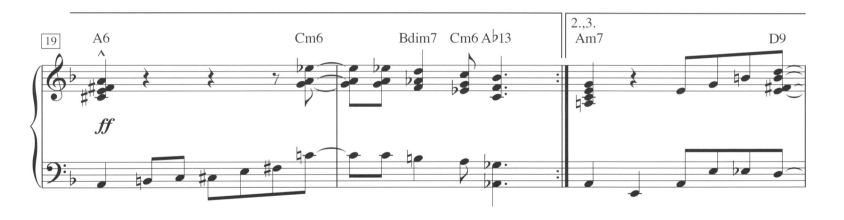

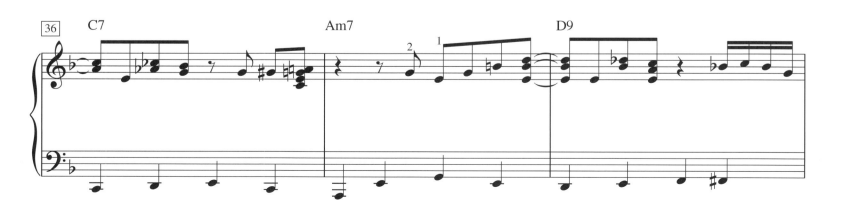

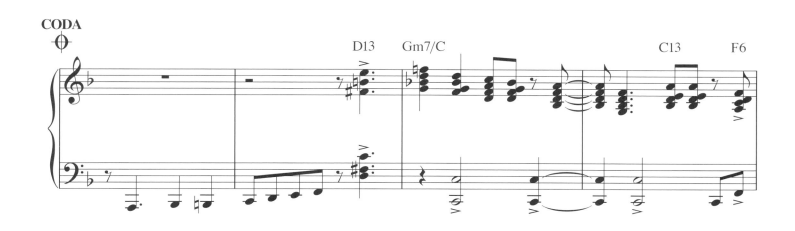

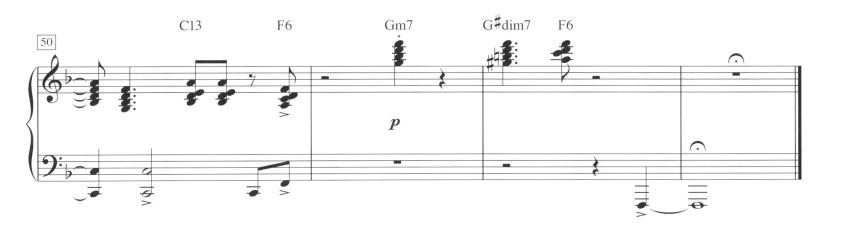

SIPPIN' AT BELLS

By MILES DAVIS

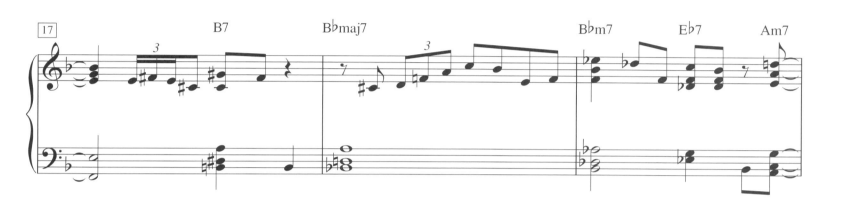

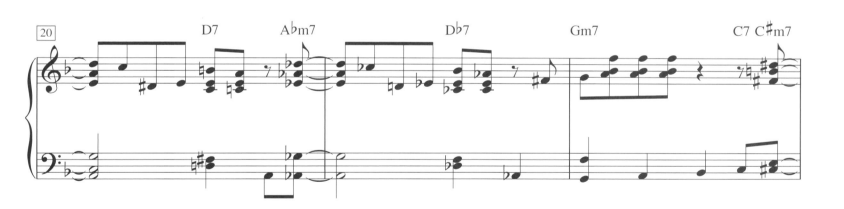

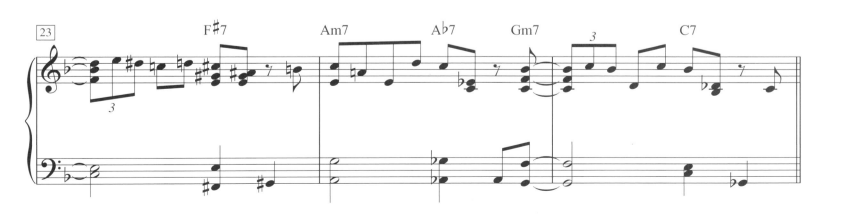

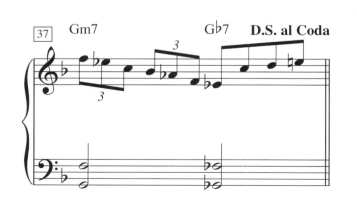

SO WHAT

By MILES DAVIS

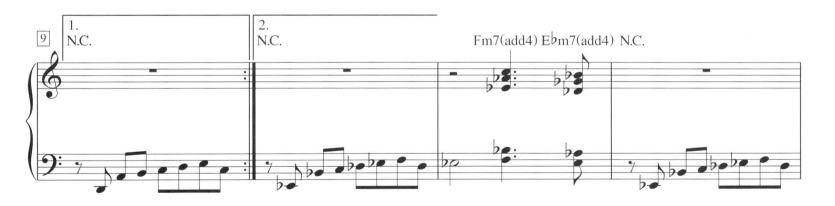

SOME OTHER SPRING

Words and Music by ARTHUR HERZOG, JR.
and IRENE KITCHINGS

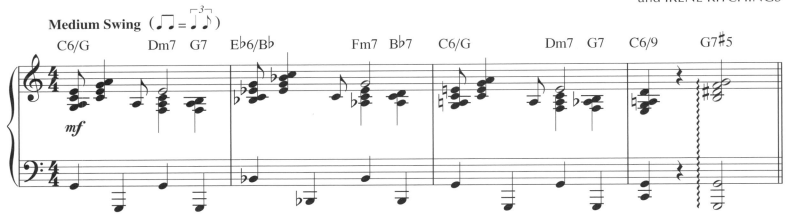

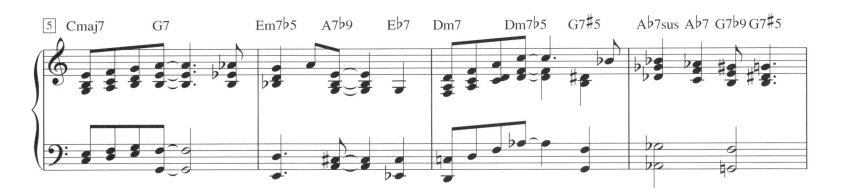

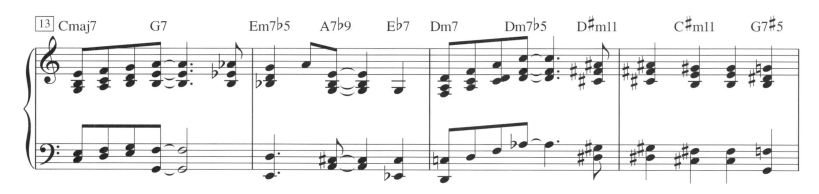

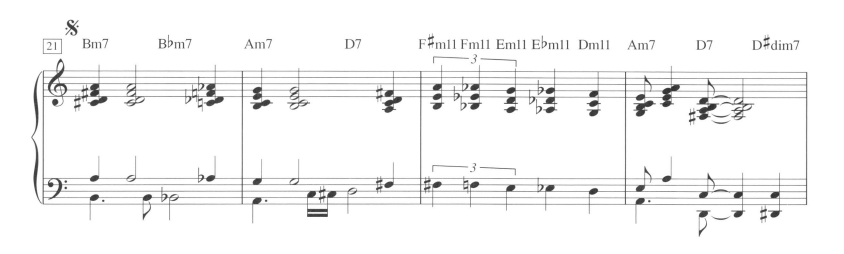

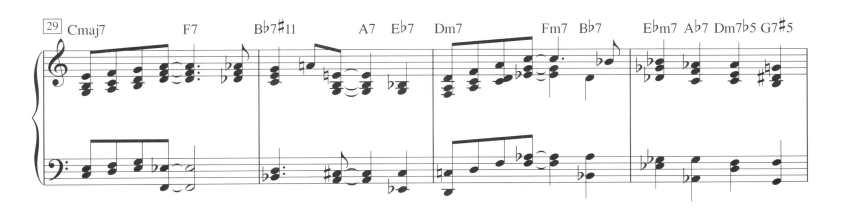

SONG FOR MY FATHER

Words and Music by
HORACE SILVER

STOLEN MOMENTS

Words and Music by
OLIVER NELSON

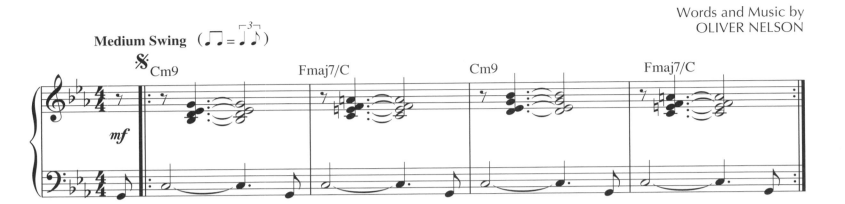

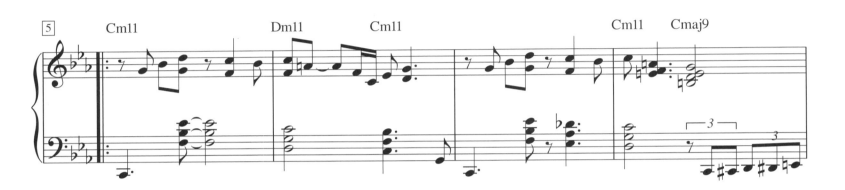

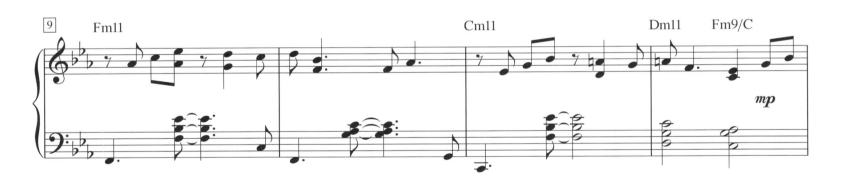

THINGS AIN'T WHAT THEY USED TO BE

By MERCER ELLINGTON

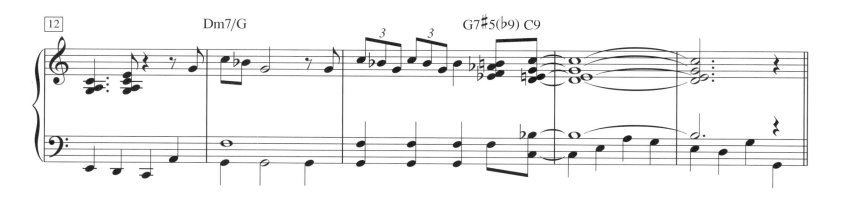

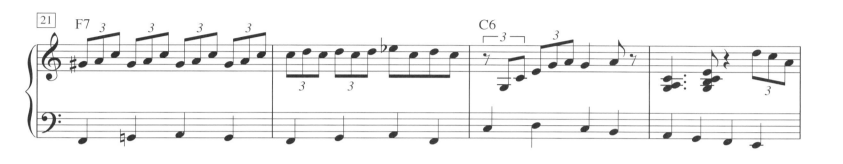

TURNAROUND

By ORNETTE COLEMAN

TOPSY

Written by EDGAR BATTLE
and EDDIE DURHAM

Fast Swing

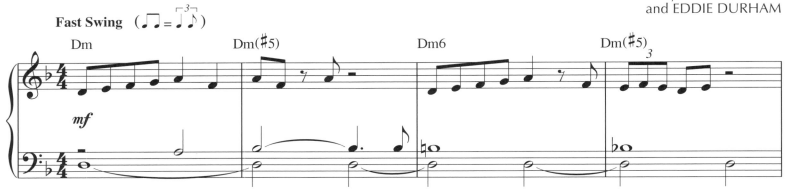

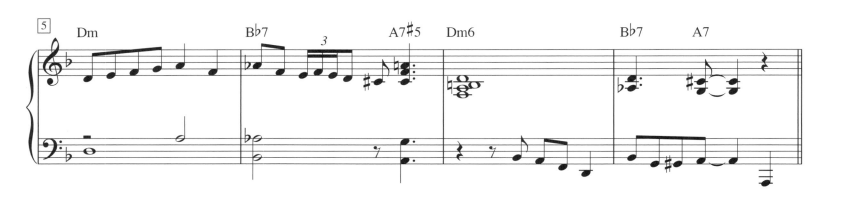

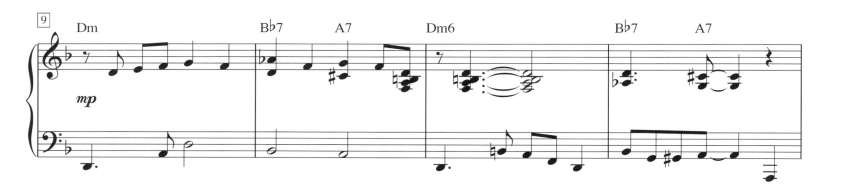

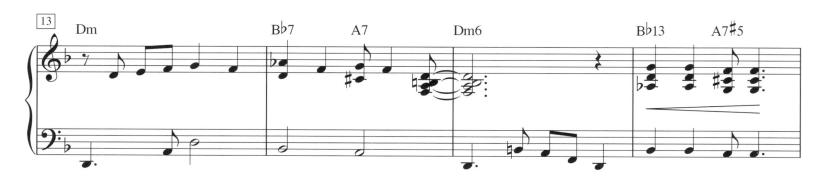

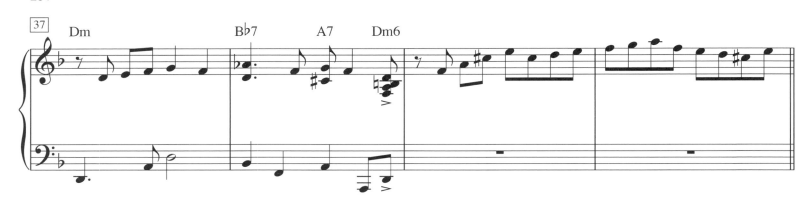

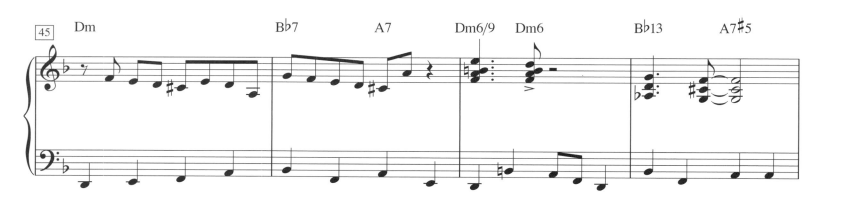

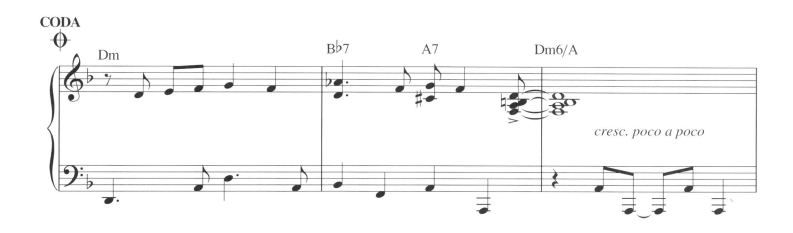

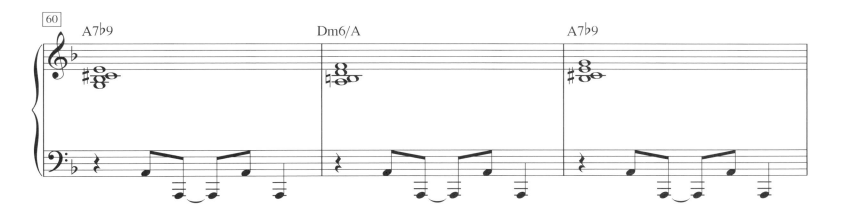

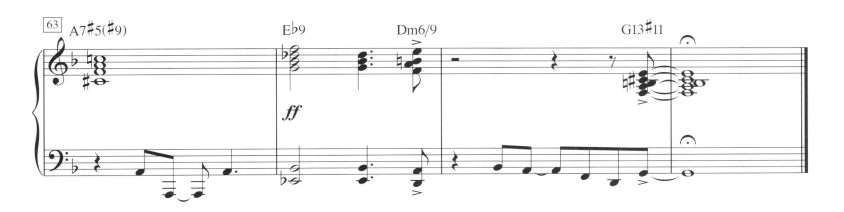

TUNE UP

By MILES DAVIS

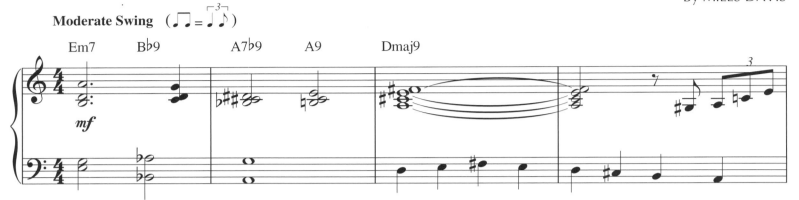

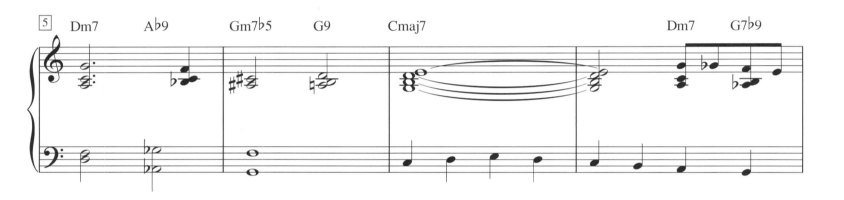

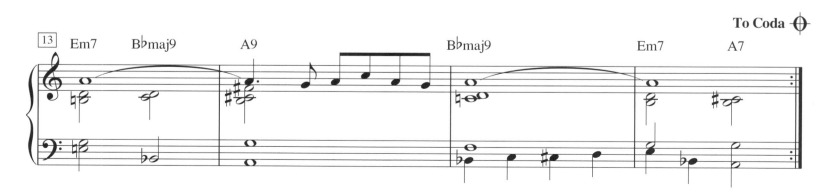

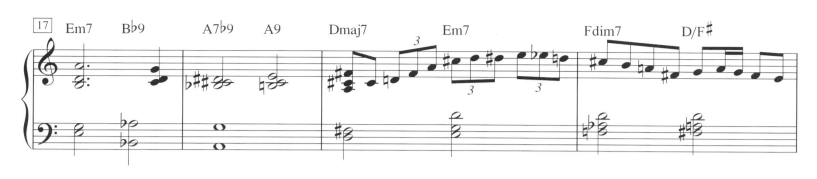

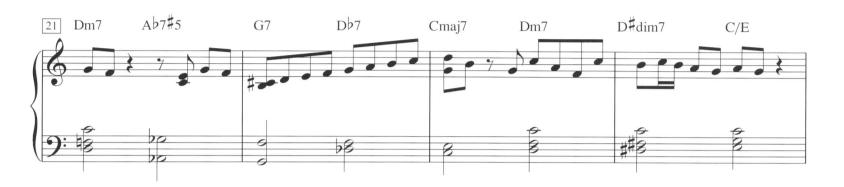

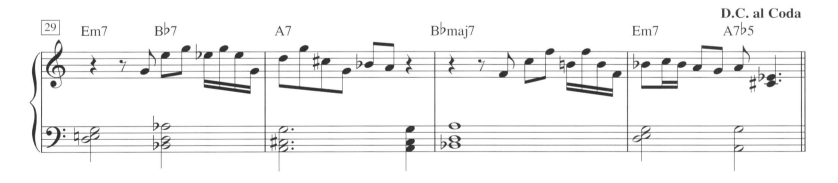

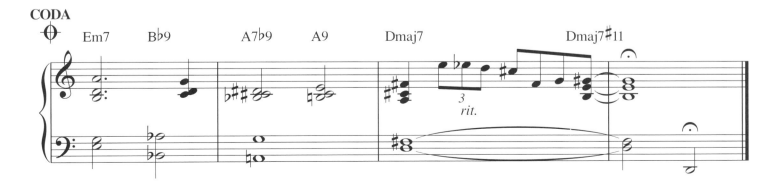

UN POCO LOCO

By EARL "BUD" POWELL

Fast Latin

WEST COAST BLUES

By JOHN L. (WES) MONTGOMERY

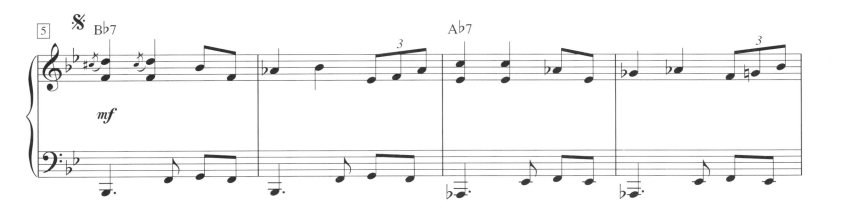

UP JUMPED SPRING

By FREDDIE HUBBARD

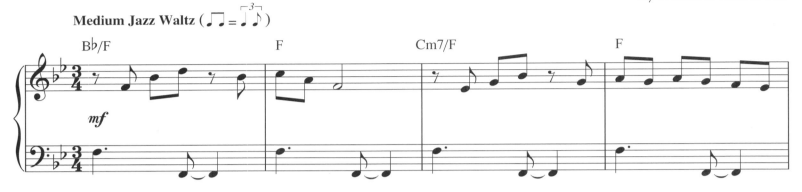

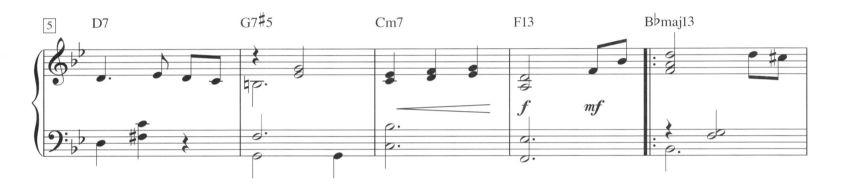

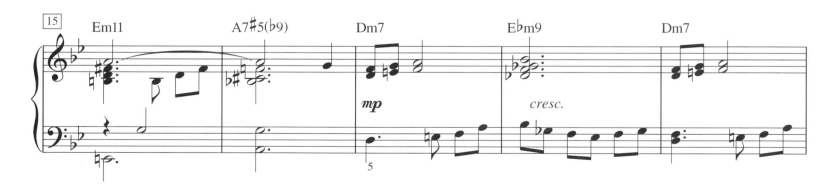

WATERMELON MAN

By HERBIE HANCOCK

WHAT AM I HERE FOR?

By DUKE ELLINGTON

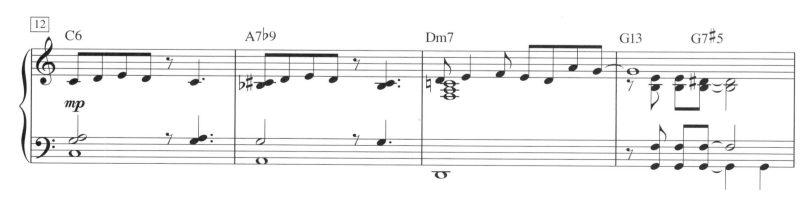

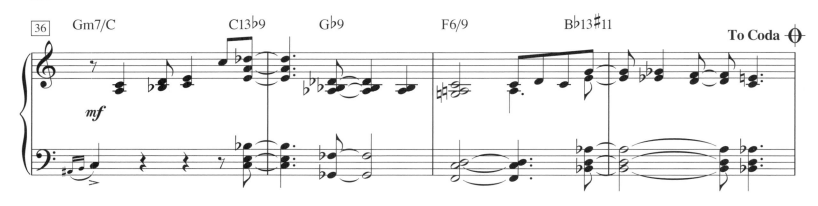

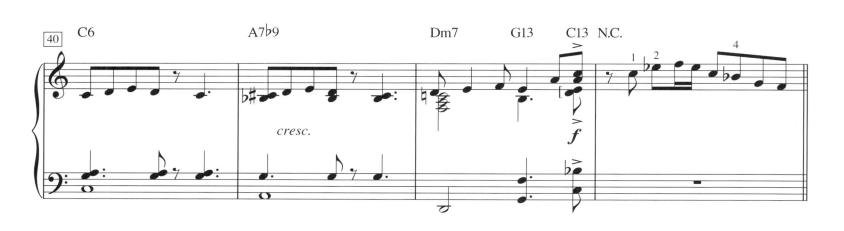

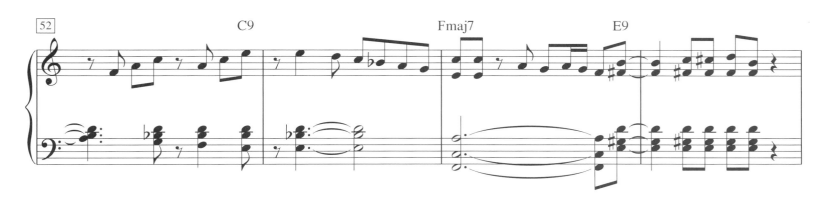

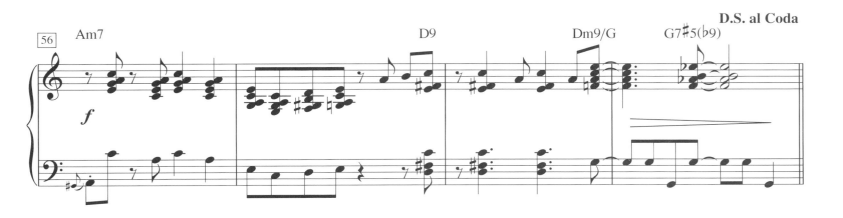

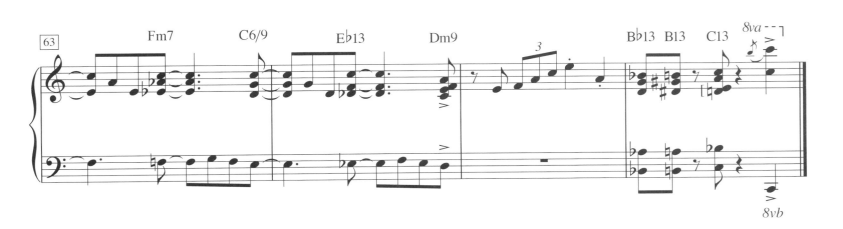

YARDBIRD SUITE

By CHARLIE PARKER

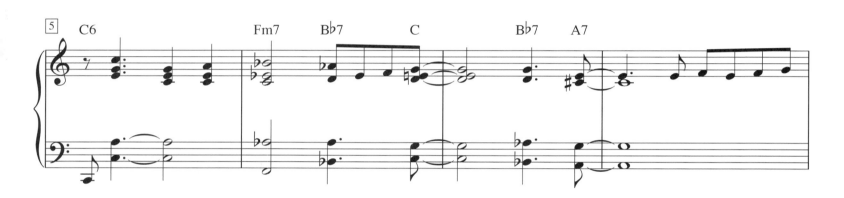

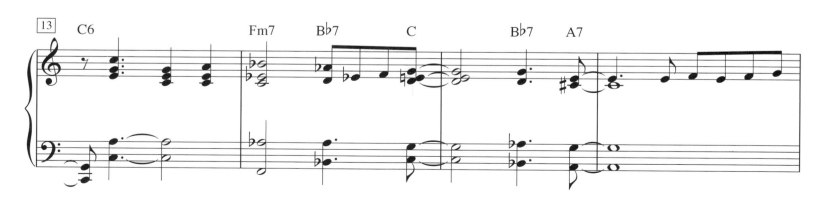

WHISPER NOT

By BENNY GOLSON

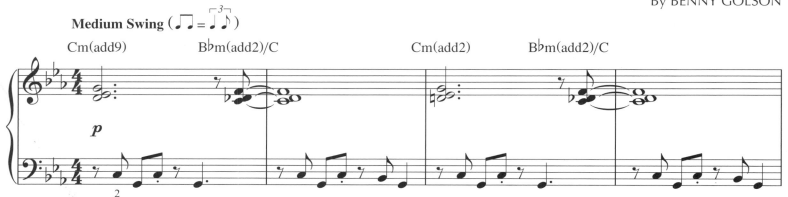

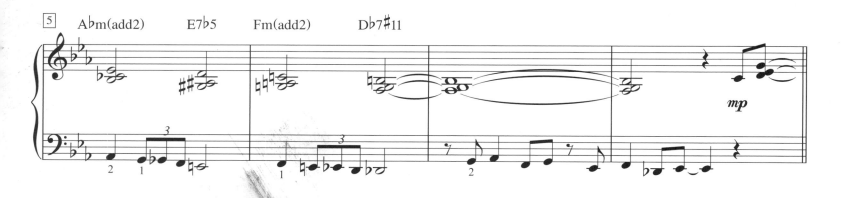

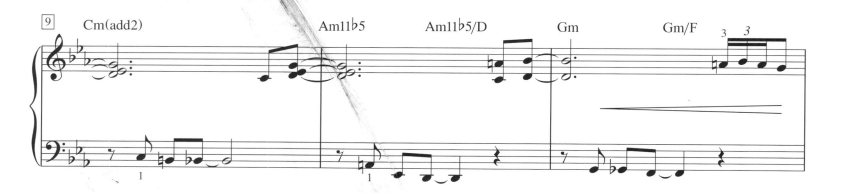

312

THE BEST EVER

COLLECTION
ARRANGED FOR PIANO, VOICE AND GUITAR

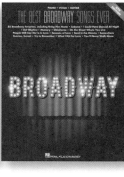

150 OF THE MOST BEAUTIFUL SONGS EVER
00360735 150 ballads............................$32.99

BEST ACOUSTIC ROCK SONGS EVER
00310984 65 acoustic hits.....................$22.99

MORE OF THE BEST ACOUSTIC ROCK SONGS EVER
00311738 69 songs..............................$19.95

BEST BIG BAND SONGS EVER
00286933 66 favorites $19.99

BEST BLUES SONGS EVER
00312874 73 blues tunes $19.99

BEST BROADWAY SONGS EVER - 6TH EDITION
00291992 85 songs..............................$24.99

MORE OF THE BEST BROADWAY SONGS EVER
00311501 82 songs..............................$22.95

BEST CHILDREN'S SONGS EVER
00159272 101 songs.............................$19.99

BEST CHRISTMAS SONGS EVER
00359130 69 holiday favorites...............$27.50

BEST CLASSIC ROCK SONGS EVER
00289313 64 hits $24.99

THE BEST COUNTRY ROCK SONGS EVER
00118881 52 hits $19.99

THE BEST CONTEMPORARY CHRISTIAN SONGS EVER – 2ND EDITION
00311985 ....$21.99

BEST COUNTRY SONGS EVER
00359135 76 classic country hits...........$22.99

BEST DISCO SONGS EVER
00312565 50 songs..............................$19.99

THE BEST DIXIELAND SONGS EVER
00312326 ....$19.99

BEST EARLY ROCK 'N' ROLL SONGS EVER
00310816 74 songs..............................$19.95

BEST EASY LISTENING SONGS EVER
00359193 75 mellow favorites...............$22.99

BEST FOLK/POP SONGS EVER
00138299 66 hits $19.99

BEST GOSPEL SONGS EVER
00310503 80 gospel songs.....................$19.99

BEST HYMNS EVER
00310774 118 hymns $18.99

BEST JAZZ STANDARDS EVER
00311641 77 jazz hits...........................$22.99

BEST LATIN SONGS EVER
00310355 67 songs..............................$19.99

BEST LOVE SONGS EVER
00359198 62 favorite love songs...........$19.99

THE BEST MOVIE SONGS EVER SONGBOOK – 5TH EDITION
00291062 75 songs..............................$24.99

BEST MOVIE SOUNDTRACK SONGS EVER
00146161 70 songs..............................$19.99

BEST POP/ROCK SONGS EVER
00138279 50 classics $19.99

BEST PRAISE & WORSHIP SONGS EVER
00311057 80 all-time favorites...............$22.99

BEST R&B SONGS EVER
00310184 66 songs..............................$19.95

BEST ROCK SONGS EVER
00490424 63 songs..............................$18.95

BEST SONGS EVER
00265721 71 must-own classics $24.99

BEST SOUL SONGS EVER
00311427 70 hits $19.95

BEST STANDARDS EVER, VOL. 1 (A-L)
00359231 72 beautiful ballads..............$17.95

BEST STANDARDS EVER, VOL. 2 (M-Z)
00359232 73 songs..............................$17.99

MORE OF THE BEST STANDARDS EVER – VOL. 2 (M-Z) – 2ND EDITION
00310814 ....$17.95

BEST WEDDING SONGS EVER
00290985 70 songs..............................$24.99

HAL•LEONARD®
Visit us online
for complete songlists at
www.halleonard.com

jazz piano solos series

Each volume features exciting new arrangements with chord symbols of the songs which helped define a style.

vol. 1 miles davis
00306521.....................$19.99

vol. 2 jazz blues
00306522.....................$19.99

vol. 3 latin jazz
00310621.....................$19.99

vol. 4 bebop jazz
00310709.....................$19.99

vol. 5 cool jazz
00310710.....................$17.99

vol. 6 hard bop
00323507.....................$16.99

vol. 7 smooth jazz
00310727.....................$19.99

vol. 8 jazz pop
00311786.....................$19.99

vol. 9 duke ellington
00311787.....................$19.99

vol. 10 jazz ballads
00311788.....................$19.99

vol. 11 soul jazz
00311789.....................$17.99

vol. 12 swinging jazz
00311797.....................$19.99

vol. 13 jazz gems
00311899.....................$17.99

vol. 14 jazz classics
00311900.....................$19.99

vol. 15 bossa nova
00311906.....................$17.99

vol. 16 disney
00312121.....................$19.99

vol. 17 antonio carlos jobim
00312122.....................$19.99

vol. 18 modern jazz quartet
00307270.....................$16.99

vol. 19 bill evans
00307273.....................$19.99

vol. 20 gypsy jazz
00307289.....................$19.99

vol. 21 new orleans
00312169.....................$17.99

vol. 22 classic jazz
00001529.....................$17.99

vol. 23 jazz for lovers
00312548.....................$19.99

vol. 24 john coltrane
00307395.....................$19.99

vol. 25 christmas songs
00101790.....................$17.99

vol. 26 george gershwin
00103353.....................$19.99

vol. 27 late night jazz
00312547.....................$19.99

vol. 28 the beatles
00119302.....................$19.99

vol. 29 elton john
00120968.....................$19.99

vol. 30 cole porter
00123364.....................$19.99

vol. 31 cocktail piano
00123366.....................$19.99

vol. 32 johnny mercer
00123367.....................$16.99

vol. 33 gospel
00127079.....................$19.99

vol. 34 horace silver
00139633.....................$16.99

vol. 35 stride piano
00139685.....................$17.99

vol. 36 broadway jazz
00144365.....................$19.99

vol. 37 silver screen jazz
00144366.....................$17.99

vol. 38 henry mancini
00146382.....................$19.99

vol. 39 sacred christmas carols
00147678.....................$17.99

vol. 40 charlie parker
00149089.....................$16.99

vol. 41 pop standards
00153656.....................$17.99

vol. 42 dave brubeck
00154634.....................$17.99

vol. 43 candlelight jazz
00154901.....................$17.99

vol. 44 jazz standards
00160856.....................$19.99

vol. 45 christmas standards
00172024.....................$19.99

vol. 46 cocktail jazz
00172025.....................$19.99

vol. 47 hymns
00172026.....................$17.99

vol. 48 blue skies & other irving berlin songs
00197873.....................$19.99

vol. 49 thelonious monk
00232767.....................$16.99

vol. 50 best smooth jazz
00233277.....................$16.99

vol. 51 disney favorites
00233315.....................$19.99

vol. 52 bebop classics
00234075.....................$16.99

vol. 53 jazz-rock
00256715.....................$16.99

vol. 54 jazz fusion
00256716.....................$16.99

vol. 55 ragtime
00274961.....................$16.99

vol. 56 pop ballads
00274962.....................$16.99

vol. 57 pat metheny
00277058.....................$19.99

vol. 58 big band era
00284837.....................$17.99

vol. 59 west coast jazz
00290792.....................$17.99

vol. 60 boogie woogie
00363280.....................$17.99

vol. 61 christmas classics
00367872.....................$17.99

vol. 62 coffee table jazz
00379205.....................$19.99

vol. 63 classical jazz
00428375.....................$19.99

Hal•Leonard®

Visit Hal Leonard Online at
www.halleonard.com

Prices, contents & availability subject to change without notice. 0822
427

Expand Your Jazz Piano Technique

BLUES, JAZZ & ROCK RIFFS FOR KEYBOARDS
by William T. Eveleth
Because so much of today's popular music has its roots in blues, the material included here is a vital component of jazz, rock, R&B, gospel, soul, and even pop. The author has compiled actual licks, riffs, turnaround phrases, embellishments, and basic patterns that define good piano blues and can be used as a basis for players to explore and create their own style.
00221028 Book..$11.95

BOOGIE WOOGIE FOR BEGINNERS
by Frank Paparelli
This bestseller is now available with a CD of demonstration tracks! A short easy method for learning to play boogie woogie, designed for the beginner and average pianist. Includes: exercises for developing left-hand bass; 25 popular boogie woogie bass patterns; arrangements of "Down the Road a Piece" and "Answer to the Prayer" by well-known pianists; a glossary of musical terms for dynamics, tempo and style; and more.
00312559 Book/CD Pack $14.99

A CLASSICAL APPROACH TO JAZZ PIANO IMPROVISATION
by Dominic Alldis
This keyboard instruction book is designed for the person who was trained classically but wants to expand into the very exciting — yet very different — world of jazz improvisation. Author Dominic Alldis provides clear explanations and musical examples of: pentatonic improvisation; the blues; rock piano; rhythmic placement; scale theory; major, minor and pentatonic scale theory applications; and more.
00310979 Book...............................$16.95

THE HARMONY OF BILL EVANS
by Jack Reilly
A compilation of articles — now revised and expanded — that originally appeared in the quarterly newsletter *Letter from Evans*, this unique folio features extensive analysis of Evans' work. Pieces examined include: B Minor Waltz • Funny Man • How Deep Is the Ocean • I Fall in Love Too Easily • I Should Care • Peri's Scope • Time Remembered • and Twelve Tone Tune.
00699405 Book...............................$19.99

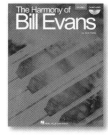

THE HARMONY OF BILL EVANS - VOLUME 2
by Jack Reilly
Reilly's second volume includes two important theory chapters, plus ten of Bill's most passionate and melodically gorgeous works. The accompanying audio CD will add to the enjoyment, understanding, and appreciation of the written examples. Songs include: For Nenette • January • Laurie • Maxine • Song for Helen • Turn Out the Stars • Very Early • Waltz for Debby • and more.
00311828 Book/CD Pack $29.99

AN INTRODUCTION TO JAZZ CHORD VOICING FOR KEYBOARD - 2ND EDITION
by Bill Boyd
This book is designed for the pianist/keyboardist with moderate technical skills and reading ability who desires to play jazz styles and learn to improvise from reading chord symbols. It is an ideal self-teaching book for keyboardists in high school and junior high jazz ensembles. Unique features of this book include chords and progressions written out in all keys, a simple fingering system which applies to all keys, and coverage of improvising and solo playing.
00854100 Book/CD Pack...............................$19.95

INTROS, ENDINGS & TURNAROUNDS FOR KEYBOARD
ESSENTIAL PHRASES FOR SWING, LATIN, JAZZ WALTZ, AND BLUES STYLES
by John Valerio
Learn the intros, endings and turnarounds that all of the pros know and use! This new keyboard instruction book by John Valerio covers swing styles, ballads, Latin tunes, jazz waltzes, blues, major and minor keys, vamps and pedal tones, and more.
00290525 Book...............................$12.95

JAZZ ETUDE INSPIRATIONS
EIGHT PIANO ETUDES INSPIRED BY THE MASTERS
by Jeremy Siskind
Etudes in the style of legendary greats Oscar Peterson, Duke Ellington, McCoy Tyner, Jelly Roll Morton, Chick Corea, Brad Mehldau, Count Basie and Herbie Hancock will help students master some technical challenges posed by each artist's individual style. The performance notes include a biography, practice tips and a list of significant recordings. Tunes include: Count on Me • Hand Battle • Jelly Roll Me Home • Minor Tyner • Oscar's Bounce • Pineapple Woman • Repeat After Me • Tears Falling on Still Water.
00296860 Book...............................$8.99

JAZZ PIANO
by Liam Noble
Featuring lessons, music, historical analysis and rare photos, this book/CD pack provides a complete overview of the techniques and styles popularized by 15 of the greatest jazz pianists of all time. All the best are here: from the early ragtime stylings of Ferdinand "Jelly Roll" Morton, to the modal escapades of Bill Evans, through the '70s jazz funk of Herbie Hancock. CD contains 15 full-band tracks.
00311050 Book/CD Pack $19.99

JAZZ PIANO CONCEPTS & TECHNIQUES
by John Valerio
This book provides a step-by-step approach to learning basic piano realizations of jazz and pop tunes from lead sheets. Systems for voicing chords are presented from the most elementary to the advanced along with methods for practicing each system. Both the non-jazz and the advanced jazz player will benefit from the focus on: chords, chord voicings, harmony, melody and accompaniment, and styles.
00290490 Book...............................$18.99

JAZZ PIANO TECHNIQUE
by John Valerio
This one-of-a-kind book applies traditional technique exercises to specific jazz piano needs. Topics include: scales (major, minor, chromatic, pentatonic, etc.), arpeggios (triads, seventh chords, upper structures), finger independence exercises (static position, held notes, Hanon exercises), and more! The audio includes 45 recorded examples.
00312059 Book/Online Audio.....................$19.99

JAZZ PIANO VOICINGS
by Rob Mullins
Long-time performer and educator Rob Mullins helps players enter the jazz world by providing voicings that will help the player develop skills in the jazz genre and start sounding professional right away — without years of study! Includes a "Numeric Voicing Chart," chord indexes in all 12 keys, info about what range of the instrument you can play chords in, and a beginning approach to bass lines.
00310914 Book.....................$19.95

HAL•LEONARD®
CORPORATION
7777 W. BLUEMOUND RD. P.O. BOX 13819 MILWAUKEE, WI 53213
www.halleonard.com

1015

NOTE-FOR-NOTE
KEYBOARD TRANSCRIPTIONS

These outstanding collections feature note-for-note transcriptions from the artists who made the songs famous. They're perfect for performers or students who want to play just like their keyboard idols!

ACOUSTIC PIANO BALLADS
16 acoustic piano favorites: Angel • Candle in the Wind • Don't Let the Sun Go Down on Me • Endless Love • Imagine • It's Too Late • Let It Be • Mandy • Ribbon in the Sky • Sailing • She's Got a Way • So Far Away • Tapestry • You Never Give Me Your Money • You've Got a Friend • Your Song.
00690351.............................$19.95

THE BEATLES KEYBOARD BOOK
23 Beatles favorites, including: All You Need Is Love • Back in the U.S.S.R. • Come Together • Get Back • Good Day Sunshine • Hey Jude • Lady Madonna • Let It Be • Lucy in the Sky with Diamonds • Ob-La-Di, Ob-La-Da • Oh! Darling • Penny Lane • Revolution • We Can Work It Out • With a Little Help from My Friends • and more.
00694827.............................$24.99

CLASSIC ROCK
35 all-time rock classics: Beth • Bloody Well Right • Changes • Cold as Ice • Come Sail Away • Don't Do Me like That • Hard to Handle • Heaven • Killer Queen • King of Pain • Layla • Light My Fire • Oye Como Va • Piano Man • Takin' Care of Business • Werewolves of London • and more.
00310940.............................$29.99

COLDPLAY
A dozen of the best from the British band: Amsterdam • Atlas • Clocks • Death and All His Friends • Fix You • For You • Paradise • The Scientist • A Sky Full of Stars • Speed of Sound • Violet Hill • Viva La Vida.
00141590.............................$24.99

DREAM THEATER – SELECTIONS FROM THE ASTONISHING
14 exact transcriptions: Dystopian Overture • The Gift of Music • Lord Nafaryus • Moment of Betrayal • My Last Farewell • Ravenskill • A Tempting Offer • When Your Time Has Come • and more.
00192244.............................$19.99

JAZZ
24 favorites from Bill Evans, Thelonious Monk, Oscar Peterson, Bud Powell, Art Tatum and more. Includes: Ain't Misbehavin' • April in Paris • Autumn in New York • Body and Soul • Freddie Freeloader • Giant Steps • My Funny Valentine • Satin Doll • Song for My Father • Stella by Starlight • and more.
00310941.............................$24.99

JAZZ STANDARDS
23 classics by 23 jazz masters, including: Blue Skies • Come Rain or Come Shine • Honeysuckle Rose • I Remember You • A Night in Tunisia • Stormy Weather (Keeps Rainin' All the Time) • Where or When • and more.
00311731.............................$29.99

THE BILLY JOEL KEYBOARD BOOK
16 mega-hits from the Piano Man himself: Allentown • And So It Goes • Honesty • Just the Way You Are • Movin' Out • My Life • New York State of Mind • Piano Man • Pressure • She's Got a Way • Tell Her About It • and more.
00694828.............................$24.99

BILLY JOEL FAVORITES
Here are 18 of the very best from Billy: Don't Ask Me Why • The Entertainer • 52nd Street • An Innocent Man • Lullabye (Goodnight, My Angel) • Only the Good Die Young • Say Goodbye to Hollywood • Vienna • and more.
00691060.............................$29.99

THE ELTON JOHN KEYBOARD BOOK
20 of Elton John's best songs: Bennie and the Jets • Candle in the Wind • Crocodile Rock • Daniel • Don't Let the Sun Go Down on Me • Goodbye Yellow Brick Road • I Guess That's Why They Call It the Blues • Little Jeannie • Rocket Man • Your Song • and more.
00694829.............................$27.99

ELTON JOHN FAVORITES
Here are Elton's keyboard parts for 20 top songs: Can You Feel the Love Tonight • I'm Still Standing • Indian Sunset • Levon • Madman Across the Water • Pinball Wizard • Sad Songs (Say So Much) • Saturday Night's Alright (For Fighting) • and more.
00691059.............................$27.99

KEYBOARD INSTRUMENTALS
22 songs transcribed exactly as you remember them, including: Alley Cat • Celestial Soda Pop • Green Onions • The Happy Organ • Last Date • Miami Vice • Outa-Space • Popcorn • Red River Rock • Tubular Bells • and more.
00109769.............................$19.99

ALICIA KEYS
Authentic piano and vocal transcriptions of 18 of her best-known songs, including: Fallin' • How Come You Don't Call Me • If I Ain't Got You • No One • Prelude to a Kiss • Wild Horses • A Woman's Worth • You Don't Know My Name • and more.
00307096 ....$24.99

HAL•LEONARD®

Visit Hal Leonard online at
www.halleonard.com

Prices, contents and availability subject to change without notice.

THE CAROLE KING KEYBOARD BOOK
16 of King's greatest songs: Beautiful • Been to Canaan • Home Again • I Feel the Earth Move • It's Too Late • Jazzman • (You Make Me Feel) Like a Natural Woman • Nightingale • Smackwater Jack • So Far Away • Sweet Seasons • Tapestry • Way Over Yonder • Where You Lead • Will You Love Me Tomorrow • You've Got a Friend.
00690554.............................$24.99

JON LORD – KEYBOARDS & ORGAN ANTHOLOGY
14 from the Hammond organ pioneer, including: Burn • Child in Time • Fireball • Here I Go Again • Highway Star • Hush • Lazy • Perfect Strangers • Rubber Monkey • Smoke on the Water • Space Truckin' • Woman from Tokyo • and more.
00125865.............................$24.99

POP/ROCK
35 songs, including: Africa • Against All Odds • Axel F • Centerfold • Chariots of Fire • Cherish • Don't Let the Sun Go Down on Me • Drops of Jupiter (Tell Me) • Faithfully • It's Too Late • Just the Way You Are • Let It Be • Mandy • Sailing • Sweet Dreams Are Made of This • Walking in Memphis • and more.
00310939.............................$24.99

QUEEN
13 note-for-note transcriptions from the original recordings, including: Bohemian Rhapsody • Good Old-Fashioned Lover Boy • Killer Queen • Play the Game • Seven Seas of Rhye • Somebody to Love • We Are the Champions • You're My Best Friend • and more.
00141589.............................$24.99

ROCK HITS
30 smash hits transcribed precisely as they were played. Includes: Baba O'Riley • Bennie and the Jets • Carry On Wayward Son • Dreamer • Eye in the Sky • I Feel the Earth Move • Jump • Layla • Movin' Out (Anthony's Song) • Tempted • What a Fool Believes • You're My Best Friend • and more.
00311914 ....$29.99

ROCK KEYBOARD/ORGAN HITS
29 note-for-note transcriptions for keyboard/organ from the original recordings that made them famous: Born to Be Wild • Dirty Work • Gimme Some Lovin' • Highway Star • In-A-Gadda-Da-Vida • Like a Rolling Stone • and more.
00142488.............................$29.99

STEVIE WONDER
14 of Stevie's most popular songs: Boogie on Reggae Woman • Hey Love • Higher Ground • I Wish • Isn't She Lovely • Lately • Living for the City • Overjoyed • Ribbon in the Sky • Send One Your Love • Superstition • That Girl • You Are the Sunshine of My Life • You Haven't Done Nothin'.
00306698.............................$24.99